COMMON AUSTRALIAN FUNGI

A BUSHWALKER'S GUIDE

Revised edition

TONY YOUNG

Line drawings by Tony Young
Watercolours by Kay Smith

UNSW PRESS

A UNSW Press book

Published by
University of New South Wales Press Ltd
University of New South Wales
Sydney 2052 Australia
www.unswpress.com.au

© A.M. Young
First published in 1982
Reprinted with minor corrections 1986
Second edition 1994
Revised edition 2000

This book is copyright. Apart from any fair dealing
for the purpose of private study, research, criticism
or review, as permitted under the Copyright Act,
no part may be reproduced by any process without
written permission. Inquiries should be addressed
to the publisher.

National Library of Australia
Cataloguing-in-Publication entry:

   Young, Tony, 1943–.
   Common Australian fungi: a bushwalker's guide.

   Revised ed.
   Bibliography.
   Includes index.
   ISBN 0 86840 650 3.

   1. Fungi – Australia – Identification. I. Title.

   579.50994

Printer BPA, Melbourne

CONTENTS

ACKNOWLEDGEMENTS

The author would like to thank the following people who kindly gave permission to use their photographic material: Mr George Groves (*Podaxis carcinomalis*) and Mr John Hunter (*Cyptotrama asprata* and *Ramariopsis sp.*). In addition a special thank you to my wife Dorothy who, as always, provided the encouragement to continue.

INTRODUCTION

People often ask: 'Why study fungi?' 'What use are they?' This is because most people have little idea of the importance of fungi and even less incentive to find out. Admittedly, fungi have pretty awful press: they only seem to be noticed when a poisoning has occurred and the victim's symptoms luridly described. With such negative attitudes in the community, it is small wonder that the average person is neither very interested nor sees any benefit in the study of the fungi.

Nevertheless, the word *useful* was made for fungi, for without them, life on earth as we know it would be almost destroyed within 50 to 60 years. Fungi are the main recycling agents for most of the dead plant material produced on earth. Without them logs and plant litter would not become humus and return to the soil; without this composting action of the fungi, the rising heaps of dead plant material would steadily lock away all the earth's nutrients. Fungi are also essential to daily life, for example, beer, wine and many types of bread cannot be made without yeast. Nor can many types of cheese and some oriental foods such as soya sauce be manufactured without fungal action. Most antibiotics cannot be produced, nor organ transplants carried out without certain drugs produced by fungi. In the bushland, large numbers of our native plants would become extinct within 100 years without the fungi that live on their roots — most particularly all the species related to eucalypts, ti-trees, melaleucas, bottle-brushes and casuarinas. Some of our small native animals such as bettongs would also be seriously affected because fungi form a very important part of their diets.

Fungi are definitely worth a great deal of study. On the destructive side, the rust and smut fungi attack our crops, wood rots attack our trees, moulds compete for our stored foods, tinea and 'ring worm' attack our bodies, mildews rot our clothes, and still other fungi attack our animals or the wood structure of our homes. Even our diesel fuel and camera lenses can be food for certain sorts of exotic fungi, so that fungi are most certainly worth a great deal of study to minimise the billions of dollars worth of damage that they do each year.

FUNGI IN THE BUSHLAND

Introduction

Most of us group bushland fungi as either being 'mush-rooms' or 'toadstools'. By these terms, we suggest that one group is edible and the other is poisonous. While this idea is false, it also shows that common names for fungi rarely exist, consequently this book uses the scientific names wherever possible.

There are many hundreds of species of microfungi but these can only be examined under a microscope and so are not dealt with here. Only the larger fungi, frequently noticed during an autumn stroll, are considered. Three groups of fungi comprise most of the 'mushrooms and toadstools' of the bushland and these are outlined below.

Myxomycetes (Slime-moulds)

These generally tiny plants are very common, but they are so small and grow in such sheltered places that they are readily overlooked. They are visible to the naked eye.

Upon germination, a cell emerges from a slime-mould spore. The cell begins to crawl actively over the sub-strate, rather like an amoeba, and feeds on bacteria. It reproduces by simple fission and rapidly produces hun-dreds of cells. Eventually a chemical signal stops the feeding activity in all the cells, and they begin to flow together towards a central point. At the central point, the cells combine to produce the sporophore for that partic-ular slime-mould species.

Figure 1 Typical Myxomycene Sporophores

Stemonitis   Lycogala   Arcyriia   Dictydium

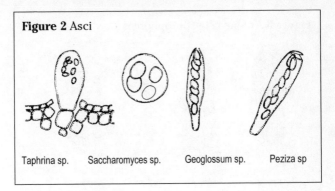

Figure 2 Asci

Taphrina sp. Saccharomyces sp. Geoglossum sp. Peziza sp

Myxomycetes are common in damp places such as the undersides of logs. They cause few serious plant diseases (a notable exception is club-root of the cabbage family produced by *Plasmodiophora brassicae*) and primarily assist in the breakdown of organic matter. A single, large species called *Fuligo septica* is mentioned in this book.

Ascomycetes (Sack-fungi)

In order for a fungal species to be an Ascomycete, it must produce an ascus at some stage of its life cycle. Asci are illustrated in Figure 2 above. The fungal spores lie in the ascus rather like peas in a pod. The most common number of spores per ascus is 8 but sometimes there may be only 4 (e.g. yeasts). Other species may produce 16, 32, 64, 128, or an indeterminate number.

Asci release their spores in a variety of ways: there may be a small removable cap called an operculum; there may be a terminal pore or slit through which the spores are squirted; or the ascal wall may simply disintegrate to release the spores. Sometimes the asci are exposed directly to the air in a fruiting structure called an apothecium; at other times they are enclosed in a flask-like structure called a perithecium.

Many Ascomycetes are important to human life. Yeasts are used in the production of bread and fermented drinks; penicillin is produced by a member of the Ascomycetes and other species produce antibiotics. Many species of the Ascomycetes are parasitic on plants and cause severe crop damage. (Leaf-curl of peach by *Taphrina deformans* is an example.) Some Ascomycete species are quite common in the Australian bushland and several larger ones are dealt with in this book.

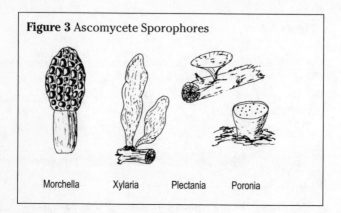

Figure 3 Ascomycete Sporophores

Morchella   Xylaria   Plectania   Poronia

Basidiomycetes (Basidia-bearing fungi)

This group is considered to contain the most highly evolved fungi. It includes the rusts and smuts of plants, the puff-balls and all their relatives, the coral fungi, the bracketfungi, the pored fungi and all the fungi with gills. All Basidiomycetes have basidia. These are cells which produce spores on special projections called sterigmata (singular sterigma).

Generally basidia resemble a club in shape, but there are variations. Some are deeply divided like a tuning fork; others look like a ping-pong bat. The most common number of spores produced on a basidium is 4, however some species produce only 2, and still others produce more than 4 spores.

Basidiomycetes are by far the most common fungi encountered in the bushland and most of the fungi described in this book belong to the Basidiomycetes.

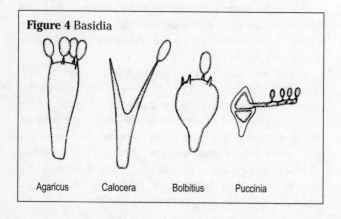

Figure 4 Basidia

Agaricus   Calocera   Bolbitius   Puccinia

Fungal Structure

The most complex members of the gilled fungi belong to the genus *Amanita* and a member of this genus is shown below. Not all gilled fungi will have all the structures present in an *Amanita* but the general shape will be the same.

The cap can be convex, flat, conical or infundibuliform (funnel-shaped) and its surface can be smooth, scaly, fibrous or slimy. Its colours may be any hue of the spectrum, although greens and blues are uncommon. The cuticle of the cap may or may not peel, but this is never a test for edibility; the deadly 'Death-Cap' does peel. The cap flesh may be thick or thin, and the texture may be anything from watery to woody. In some species the flesh changes colour on exposure to air and may become pink, red, yellow, brown, green, blue or black. Frequently, the colour disappears after a short interval.

The gills produce the spores. The attachment of the gills to the cap, as revealed by a transverse section, is very important to identification. The gills may also be variously coloured: yellows, reds, browns, pinks and blacks are common. White is very common, blues and greens are rare. The colour of the gills is not a definite indication of the spores, for several red-gilled species have white

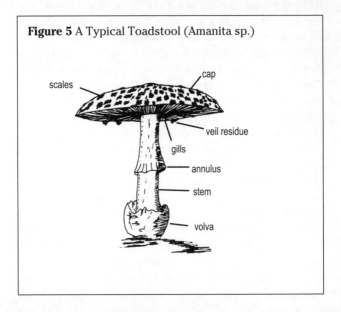

Figure 5 A Typical Toadstool (Amanita sp.)

scales
cap
veil residue
gills
annulus
stem
volva

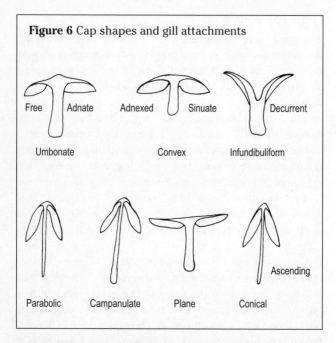

Figure 6 Cap shapes and gill attachments

spores, and one spectacular blue-gilled species has pink spores. It is always wise to make a spore-print to check on the colour 'in mass'.

The stem may be attached centrally, to one side (excentric), or it may be right at the margin (lateral). There may (or may not) be a ring or a volva. Sometimes the stem can be removed readily without gill damage.

Some Basidiomycetes have pores underneath the cap rather than gills. When identifying pored species, it is essential to know if the pores, and their associated tubes, can be easily removed from the cap. The pore attachment can be considered in the same way as the gill attachment. Another group of Basidiomycetes, the 'puffball' family or Gasteromycetes, produces an amazing diversity of sporophore structures ranging from the simple round balls of *Rhizopogon spp.* to the lacy indusium (an open mesh veil) produced by members of the genus *Dictyophora*.

Ascomycete fruiting bodies are often saucer or cup-shaped; however, the genus *Cordyceps* can produce fruiting bodies that look very like coral or clubs. Australia has the largest known species of *Cordyceps* in the world: *C. taylori*.

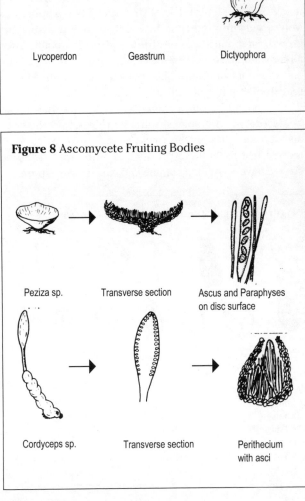

Figure 7 Gasteromycete Fruiting Bodies

Lycoperdon　　　Geastrum　　　Dictyophora

Figure 8 Ascomycete Fruiting Bodies

Peziza sp.　　　Transverse section　　　Ascus and Paraphyses on disc surface

Cordyceps sp.　　　Transverse section　　　Perithecium with asci

Spores

Spores are very small and light and they are produced in enormous numbers. An average puff-ball will liberate perhaps 25 000 000 000 spores. Counts have shown that a mushroom can liberate spores at the rate of 200 000 000 spores an hour, which means a total of 15 000 000 000 spores during its lifetime. A giant puff-ball does better, however, with an estimated total spore dispersal of 15 000 000 000 000 spores per fruiting body.

Fungi produce huge numbers of short-lived spores, in contrast to the green plants, which bear small numbers of long-lived seeds. The minute size of the spores means that they cannot contain much food material and, therefore, many die soon after release. This means that a spore has only a very limited time in which to reach a suitable growth site, and these are rare. And most suitable sites already contain fungal species competing for the nutrients and thus, out of all the billions of spores produced by a toadstool or puff-ball, only a few will survive.

Spores can be quite complicated. Their surfaces can be decorated with spines, warts or ridges, and they can also be smooth, pitted or wrinkled. Several species named in this volume produce septate spores. Some spores have an opening at one end called a germ pore.

Figure 9 Fungal Spores from Various Genera

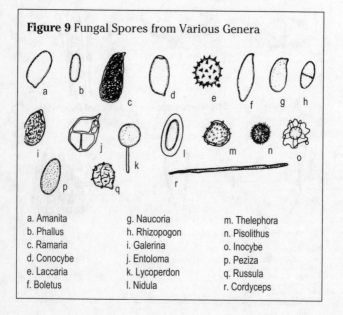

a. Amanita	g. Naucoria	m. Thelephora
b. Phallus	h. Rhizopogon	n. Pisolithus
c. Ramaria	i. Galerina	o. Inocybe
d. Conocybe	j. Entoloma	p. Peziza
e. Laccaria	k. Lycoperdon	q. Russula
f. Boletus	l. Nidula	r. Cordyceps

A solution called Melzer's Iodine is used to help in differentiating species of fungi by means of colour changes produced in the spore walls. If spores are immersed in the solution, there can be three results: there may be no change, the spores may turn brick-red, or they may turn blue-black. The two reactions are called the pseudo-amyloid (or dextrinoid) and amyloid reactions respectively.

The colours of spores are best observed by making spore-prints. To obtain a spore print, the agaric is placed, gills downwards, on black or white paper and is left for several hours while the spores are released. After the spores have settled, their colour in mass can be easily seen. Colours range from white to creams, pinks, browns and blacks. Green does occur, but it is rare.

Sclerotia

Some fungi produce a specialised resting structure called a sclerotium. The sclerotium consists of a mass of hyphae matted together and contained within a hard rind. The hyphae within the rind are generally full of food materials so that the fungus can survive an unfavourable season. Some of the species that do this are *Claviceps paspali*, *Polyporus mylittae* and *Coprinus stercoreus*. *Claviceps paspali* has a sticky, 'honey-dew' infective stage in the grass *Paspalum dilatatum*, and it is very common on paspalum seed heads during summer in Australia. *Polyporus mylittae* produces huge sclerotia that often weigh several kilogrammes. These sclerotia are sometimes turned up during ploughing, especially in mallee country. They were called 'blackfellows bread' but it is debatable whether the Aborigines ever ate such hard and gristly material. *Coprinus stercoreus* produces a brownish black sclerotium. *Polyporus tumulosus* often appears after bushfires in eucalypt woodland: it seems to need the heat stimulus of the fire to produce its large, umbrella shaped fruiting bodies growing directly on soil. These spring from a false sclerotium of mycelium and soil bound together to form a football sized mass which can be found by digging.

Many sclerotia can resist extensive drying and freezing and some will not germinate unless they have been subjected to the adverse conditions of winter, or unless a certain period of time has elapsed.

Luminescence

Some fungal species produce light through a chemical
reaction involving enzymes. The reaction is oxygen
dependent; if the fungus is deprived of air for more than a
few minutes the glow ceases. Although the causes of the
light are fairly well understood, the reasons for the production of the light by the fungus are, as yet, not definitely known. Perhaps the light attracts night-flying
insects, but this is uncertain. There are at least two
species in Australia: *Omphalotus nidiformis*, which is generally associated with trees of the genus *Eucalyptus*, and a
small, fragile species called *Mycena chlorophanus* (giving
a greenish glow), which is found in the rainforests of
Southern Queensland. *O. nidiformis* is a large sturdy
species with greyish white caps that are often streaked
with violet or black. Its favourite habitat is at the base of
living or dead gum-trees, where it can produce huge
tiered clusters up to 70 cm in diameter. It was first found
along the banks of the Swan River in Western Australia,
and may still be collected from the peppermints which
line the banks; however, it has an Australia- wide range.

Fairy Rings

The historical aspects of fairy rings are amply described
in the volume *Mushrooms and Toadstools* by J. Ramsbottom. Fairy rings have been known for many hundreds
of years. Several rings on Salisbury Plain in England are
believed to be 3 to 4 hundred years old.

Fairy rings are caused by one of several species of
ring-forming fungi that grow out radially in the soil in
search of food. As the food at the initial point is ex-
hausted, the mycelium dies and the typical ring structure
forms. The fungus then continues to grow outwards and
produces fruiting bodies under suitable conditions.

Some ring-forming species kill the grass, others do not,
but the reasons are still somewhat obscure. A current the-
ory suggests that the fungus may make the soil impervi-
ous to water and consequently the grass suffers extreme
lack of moisture. The fungal wastes are apparently effi-
cient fertilisers because the grass at the inner edge of the
ring grows much better than the normal pasture grass.

Various species in Australia form fairy rings. *Marasmius oreades* has been seen forming rings in Armidale

(New South Wales) and a species of *Agaricus* has been seen to form very large rings in playing fields at Fremantle (Western Australia). *Calvatia lilacina* is a large white puff-ball that is very common in eastern Australia and is regularly to be seen forming rings, especially on golf courses.

Fungi and Nature

Fungi do not possess chlorophyll and consequently cannot produce their own food. All fungal species (with the exception of a few aberrant forms) must, therefore, exist either as scavengers (saprophytes) or parasites. There are some species which make the best of any situation and they live saprophytically or parasitically as the food conditions permit.

Fungi are the prime destroyers of dead plant material. Unlike bacteria, which tend to remain on the surfaces of dead plants, fungi are able to grow through the dead tissues. Many species of fungi produce enzymes that soften the tissues and hasten the rotting process.

Fungal infections of plants can be highly beneficial to both the plant and the fungus. The infection site is the plant root, where a compound structure of root and fungus is formed. These structures are called mycorrhiza. Most species of plants appear to form mycorrhiza. Pine trees of the genus *Pinus* are very frequently associated with various species of the fungal genus *Boletus* but other genera, such as *Rhizopogon*, *Lactarius*, or *Amanita*, are quite common. In Australia, it is believed that *Ramaria sinapicolor* may be mycorrhizal with a range of eucalypts including the jarrah of Western Australia. *Pisolithus* spp. are also often associated with eucalypts, while the author's own observations have led him to suspect that *Pisolithus microcarpus* may form an association with the scrub box, *Tristania conferta*.

In recent years, a great deal of research has been done into the very dangerous root parasite *Phytophthora cinnamomi*, a fungus which causes the disease 'eucalyptus dieback'. The fungal spores live in mud, and so once a diseased area is identified no vehicles are permitted to travel through it so as to prevent the spores from being spread to unaffected areas. Even boots must be thoroughly washed after walking in affected areas, and the water and mud collected in special destruction pits.

FUNGI
AND PEOPLE

The Uses of Fungi

Besides the use of yeasts for bread and fermentation, fungi have long been cultivated for food. In South-East Asia the straw mushroom is grown on spent rice stalks in China and the Philippines, and the shiitake is grown on wooden poles in Japan. Both these species (as well as others) can now be bought dried in Australian shops specialising in eastern foods. In addition, fungi are used to produce certain industrial chemicals such as citric acid and of course there is large scale production of alcohol for use in engines overseas.

Other uses for fungi include production of drugs to assist in childbirth and migraine prevention, while some species have given hints of chemicals that might be useful in the fight against AIDS. Most of our Australian fungi have not yet been examined for useful chemicals, largely because there are so few people who know how to identify the larger fungi. Mycologists now have a very real fear that both our eucalypt and rainforests may be destroyed before we even find out what fungi are in them.

Some other uses for fungi include the production of beautiful dyes for cloth and insect sprays to destroy aphids in greenhouses. In forestry, fungi are used to assist tree growth. The Australian gum-tree is now grown for timber and fuel in many countries, and forestry workers from those places often visit Australia to collect the fungi growing on our gum-tree roots so that they will have the correct species of fungi for good tree growth in their own country. In England, the wood rotting species *Peniophora gigantea* helps to protect forests from other dangerous fungal parasites by rotting freshly cut surfaces before the parasites can get into the still living stump.

POISONOUS AND EDIBLE FUNGI

There is no known test by which you can tell if a fungus is edible or not. There is only one solution: the person intending to eat various species of fungi must learn to recognise the different species in the same way that one can tell the difference between edible lettuce leaves on one hand and poisonous rhubarb leaves on the other. There are, however, some good generalisations that can be made.

First, no true puff-ball genus is known to be dangerous and several are considered excellent eating. The earthball genus *Scleroderma* is definitely poisonous, but since this genus has been used to make fake truffle pâté, it can be assumed that the poison is relatively mild in very small quantities. Second, the vast majority of species are not poisonous but are not used for food because they are unpleasant to taste, are too small, or are too rare to be worth the trouble of gathering. Third, the majority of the poisonous types soon make their presence felt, usually within half an hour, and this gives a doctor time to remove the fragments from the stomach. A healthy adult is generally not in too much danger, and recovery is rapid and complete. Fourth, the very dangerous species *Amanita phalloides* which accounts for about 90 per cent of deaths from fungi poisoning in Europe, is extremely rare in Australia and occurs only on introduced species such as oaks. So far it has been seen only in Canberra and Melbourne and no deaths have resulted. About one-third of a cap of this species is quite sufficient to kill an adult.

Australia has several species of fungi containing chemicals that cause hallucinations. The dangers of using these fungi so-called 'trips' cannot be emphasised too much. One dangerous aspect is the 'flashback' where the victim suffers a hallucinatory attack as much as six months after originally eating the fungi. If this occurs while the person is driving on a freeway or in similar dangerous situation, the results could be disastrous.

Many years ago, the author accidentally ate *Agaricus xanthoderma,* recorded by Cleland (1934) as *Agaricus arvensis* var. *iodoformis.* There is an intense iodoform or phenol odour while the mushroom is being cooked and the whole cooking area is permeated by the smell. Some people have little or no discomfort, while others are violently ill. A second species, *Chlorophyllum molybdites*, is found from Sydney to Darwin. It is a large species with greenish gills, and found on lawns. It should never be eaten raw as even a mouthful will usually produce such violent stomach pain that hospital treatment will be required.

If species other than the field mushroom are to be sampled, the author suggests the following routine should be strictly adhered to:

- NEVER eat anything unless you are absolutely certain of its identity. You should aim to have the species checked out by a competent mycological authority.
- Eat only a very small amount at the first trial: you may be allergic to the species.
- Always use fresh young specimens, as most fungi tend to be a little indigestible.
- Do not drink alcohol with dishes made from the genus *Coprinus* as species belonging to this genus contain a substance similar to that used to treat alcoholics. The affected person suffers from a red flushed face and symptoms of nausea. The effects soon wear off. however, and, provided no alcohol is drunk with or soon after the meal, no ill effects occur.

Amongst the species actually eaten by the author for food are the following: *Coprinus comatus* (very good); *Boletus granulatus* (flavour good, but rather soft in texture); various species of *Agaricus* (mushrooms) which were equally good with the one exception that is detailed above; *Calvatia lilacina* (good if sliced and fried in a coating of egg and breadcrumbs); *Lactarius deliciosus* (sampled in the pickled state — may be an acquired taste).

THE STUDY OF FUNGI

Collecting Fungi

Collection of fungal material is pretty well dependent on the seasonal rains; however, it will generally be found that the main flush of activity occurs in May–June. There can be a much smaller peak in spring around September–October. The autumn flush in May–June is usually the best time to collect Basidiomycetes, but the spring flush is usually dominated by Ascomycetes. In the more tropical areas, material can be collected all year round in damp places, such as fern gullies.

After trying a number of different methods, the author's current equipment for collecting consists of:

- a small haversack;
- a camera with macro lens and colour slides;
- a small trowel, a pocket knife and a pair of tweezers;
- a note pad and pen;
- some greaseproof paper; and
- a selection of small plastic boxes including compartmentalised 'fishermen's bait boxes'.

Specimens can be placed into the boxes with the certainty that they will not be crushed. Tiny, delicate ones can go into small 'bait box' compartments, while large robust ones can be simply wrapped in greaseproof paper.

The note pad is used to record such items as data, time, location, taste, smell, substrate, colour, milk (if present), habitat, and anything at all unusual about the specimen. Some characteristics are vital to identification, but vanish rapidly as the fungus matures; these characteristics must be noted at the time of collection.

Taste is very important for identification, and even the most deadly species can be tasted provided none of the material is swallowed and the mouth is washed out afterwards or at least all saliva present is ejected. Only a piece about the size of a pea is necessary. Always, however, apply the test with caution as some species have hot, acrid flavours that can put cayenne pepper to shame.

Collect only sufficient for identification purposes and

for storing herbarium material. About fifteen or so different species in any one day is more than sufficient for most workers unless you have access to refrigeration. Spore prints should be made as soon as possible on reaching home or the laboratory. The colour of the gills should suggest the colour of the paper required.

If you intend to collect seriously, always aim to preserve a dried sample of the species collected. This will act as a reference for you and will also give future workers a chance to re-examine your findings and correct any errors you have made. Your descriptions should be made in a bound book and should be as full as possible. A transverse sectional drawing of the fungus is a great aid, and microscopical structures can be examined and drawn also.

With most species, preservation for the herbarium simply involves thorough drying and then storage with naphthalene or PDB (paradichlorobenzene). PDB is rather more toxic and needs careful use. Both substances seem rather fungicidal to moulds or mildews attacking the dried specimens. The author places his samples in tissue paper together with some naphthalene flakes. These are then placed into paper envelopes, on the outside of which are given details such as name, date of collection and habitat. Spore prints are included also.

A small dryer can be easily made out of a packing case, provided the sides have no large cracks. Two or three shelves are fitted, and a hinged door added. The shelves must be made of gauze to allow easy passage of air. A small 240 volt electric motor is then mounted at the bottom of the dryer and a very small propeller attached so that it will drive a gentle stream of air upwards over a 100 watt bulb, which is added just above the motor. Finally, air vents are cut in the top and bottom of the cabinet, and it is ready for operation. Even fairly large specimens can be thoroughly dried overnight in such a dryer.

Stains, Dyes and Reagents

There are a number of stains and reagents that are used in mycological work. The following list describes the more common ones and how they are employed.

Melzer's Iodine

20 ml distilled water

1 gm potassium iodide

$^1/_2$ gm iodine crystals

After all the above chemicals are thoroughly mixed, add 20 g of chloral hydrate. This solution is used for testing spores and certain other tissues for an amyloid or dextrinoid reaction. Amyloid tissues become blue-black; pseudo-amyloid (or dextrinoid) tissues become brick red.

Ammonia Solution

A 10 per cent solution is very useful for reconstituting dried material. Some species change colour in its presence.

Potassium Hydroxide Solution

Use a 10 per cent solution in the same way as the ammonia solution. Also used as a reagent for the fungi.

Ferrous Sulphate Solution

This produces colour changes on the flesh of many species of *Russula*. A 10 per cent solution is adequate.

Cotton-Blue Solution

Ascomycete spores display their decorations vividly if they are gently heated in a drop of this stain on a microscope slide. Mixed with lacto-phenol it is a good microscope mountant/stain. Use a *fresh* solution of 1 gm/10 ml water.

Congo-Red/Ammonia Solution

An excellent general purpose stain for fungal tissues as it stains the cell walls, not the contents. This is the stain most favoured by the author. Exact proportions are not vital, but the author finds that about enough to cover a 1 cm diameter circle dissolved into 50 ml of ammonia solution is a good working solution. It can be easily strengthened or diluted as required.

The Percussion Technique

This is used to 'splay' out material on a microscope slide so that the cellular structures can be seen. The fresh or softened material is placed on a microscope slide in a drop of mountant. A cover slip is then added. This slip is then gently tapped a few times with the end of a pencil and the tissues will spread out. Use commonsense, however; very tough tissues may require gentle pressure with the fingers.

Use of the Key

The key in the following section is designed to be used with a minimum of laboratory equipment, however, microscopical characters are added in brackets where it is felt that the more serious student can benefit. The key is arranged in the standard dichotomous form.

The user is confronted with (usually) two choices to be made about some characteristic of the fungus to be identified, for example, gills present or not. The second or more choices are marked with asterisks. Depending upon the outcome of the choice, the user is then directed by the number at the right to the next choice, located by the number on the left. The process is repeated until the generic name is reached. If the outcome is obviously

Some Orders, Families and Genera of Basidiomycetes

Tremellales   *Tremella; Tremellodon.*

Auriculariales   *Auricularia.*

Dacrymycetales *Dacrymyces; Calocera.*

Aphyllophorales *Schizophyllum; Favolus; Polyporus; Fistulina; Microporus; Fomes; Daedalea; Trametes; Cantharellus; Craterellus; Hydnum; Stereum; Thelephora; Clavicorona; Clavaria; Clavulinopsis; Ramaria; Lentinus; Lentinellus, Pycnoporus.*

Agaricales
Family 1:   Hygrophoraceae — *Hygrocybe.*
Family 2:   Tricholomataceae — *Laccaria; Clitocybe; Lepista; Tricholoma; Armillaria; Omphalina; Clitocybula; Collybia; Cyptotrama; Oudemansiella; Marasmius; Mycena; Xeromphalina.*
Family 3:   Amanitaceae — *Amanita; Volvaria; Pluteus.*
Family 4:   Agaricaceae — *Chlorophyllum; Lepiota; Agaricus.*
Family 5:   Coprinaceae — *Coprinus; Psathyrella; Panaeolus.*

wrong you may have made an error — try again.

For example, a common mushroom with gills and chocolate coloured spores would start at choice 1 (on the left) and go to choice 2. From there, choice 2(e) would direct you to choice 29 and this would give you the genus *Agaricus*. Remember though, that this book is only an introduction and you may have collected a species not covered by the book or the key.

Family 6:	Bolbitiaceae — *Conocybe; Bolbitius; Naucoria.*
Family 7:	Strophariaceae — *Stropharia; Psilocybe; Pholiota; Hypholoma.*
Family 8:	Cortinariaceae — *Inocybe; Hebeloma; Cortinarius; Descolea; Gymnopilus; Galerina.*
Family 9:	Crepidotaceae — *Crepidotus.*
Family 10:	Entolomataceae — *Entoloma.*
Family 11:	Paxillaceae — *Paxillus.*
Family 12:	Russulaceae — *Russula; Lactarius.*
Family 13:	Strobilomycetaceae — *Strobilomyces; Boletellus; Austroboletus.*
Family 14:	Boletaceae — *Boletus; Suillus.*

"Gasteromycetes"

Hymenogastrales:	*Rhizopogon.*
Phallales:	*Dictyophora; Phallus; Clathrus; Aseroe; Lysurus; Anthurus; Colus.*
Sclerodermatales:	*Scleroderma; Pisolithus.*
Lycoperdales:	*Podaxis; Geastrum; Myriostoma. Calvatia; Tulostoma; Lycoperdon.*
Nidulariales:	*Cyathus; Nidula; Crucibulum.*

Some Orders, and Genera of Ascomycetes

Clavicipitales:	*Cordyceps.*
Sphaeriales:	*Xylaria; Poronia.*
Pezizales:	*Morchella; Peziza; Cheilymenia; Plectania.*
Helotiales:	*Trichoglossum; Chlorosplenium.*

KEY
TO THE COMMON GENERA
OF AUSTRALIAN FUNGI

1   Gills present, although they may be reduced
to a series of parallel folds or wrinkles; rarely
almost absent but then the caps in tiers on a
common stem   *2*

1*   Gills not present; if a cap is present, the
undersurface may be smooth, have spines or
pores, but never gills; fungus may be variously
shaped: coralloid, cupulate, spherical, etc.   *36*

THE AGARICACEAE

2   Spore print:
      (a) white, cream or *very* faintly pink   *3*
      (b) *strongly* pink, salmon pink or salmon
          brown   *18*
      (c) green or olive green   *20*
      (d) rusty, ochre brown to cigar brown   *21*
      (e) chocolate brown   *29*
      (f) purplish to violet-black or deep black   *30*

White, cream or very faintly pink spored genera of the Agaricaceae

3   Flesh brittle and snaps like a carrot; latex may
be present; sporophores stout and intermediate
gills rare; (if plants very delicate and release a
reddish or purplish fluid only from the broken
stem, see *Mycena*). (Spores amyloid;
examination of cap tissues shows presence
of ball-shaped cells or sphaerocysts)   *4*

3*   Flesh not markedly brittle, plants stout or not;
if latex is present, it comes only from the broken
stems and the plants are then markedly delicate   *5*

4   Latex present in all parts of the fungus and
flowing readily if the plant is cut or bruised   *Lactarius*

4*   No latex present   *Russula*

5   Volva present or indications of a well
developed universal veil; ring present or not   *Amanita*

5*   Volva absent   *6*

6   On wood; brilliant yellow-orange and with
     spines/scales on the cap   *Cyptotrama*

6*   Not as above   7

7   Gills splitting along their edges; fan-shaped;
     coriaceous; always on wood; gregarious   *Schizophyllum*

7*   Gill edge serrate; cap convex, fan-shaped
     or infundibuliform; sometimes caespitose;
     usually on wood:
     (a) Spores amyloid   *Lentinellus*
     (b) No iodine reaction   *Lentinus*

7** Gill margins not serrate or splitting   8

8   Ring present:
     (a) On soil, caps usually less than 5 cm
     diameter, fragile, may be in troops,
     gills free (spores dextrinoid/pseudo-amyloid)   *Lepiota*
     (b) On soil, caps usually much greater than
     5 cm diameter, frequently 15 cm or more,
     robust, often in open pasture, gills free
     (spores dextrinoid/pseudo-amyloid)   *Macrolepiota*
     (c) On wood or at the bases of stumps, often
     in caespitose clusters, gills adnate to decurrent,
     (spores without iodine reaction)   *Armillaria*

8*   Ring not present   9

9   Gills reduced to folds or wrinkles; cap usually
     infundibuliform, or very rarely a series of
     smaller funnel-shaped caps, each one arising
     out of the top of the one below, up to
     three or four tiers   *Cantharellus*

9*   Definite gills present   10

10   Gills waxy; cap often slimy and brightly coloured
     in reds, oranges or yellows, rarely greens or lilacs;
     often hygrophanous and fragile; (spores smooth,
     no iodine reaction)   *Hygrocybe*

10* Gills pruinose; stem rather tough; in troops on
     soil; pinkish to brick coloured but a violet form is
     occasionally found; (spores globular, echinulate,
     no iodine reaction)   *Laccaria*

10** Gills neither waxy nor pruinose   *11*

11   Gills sinuate:
     (a) Spores pure white (smooth)   *Tricholoma*
     (b) Spores faintly pink (rough)   *Lepista*

11* Gills decurrent   12

11** Gills adnate, adnexed or ascending   15

12   Stipe excentric to lateral; always on wood, often

in clusters or tiers; more or less infundibuliform; one species luminous; (spores smooth, no reaction in iodine)   *Pleurotus*

12*   Stipe more or less central   *13*

13   Plant thick, fleshy with a stout stipe; always on soil; caps usually solid, convex, or umbilicate or infundibuliform; may be strongly scented   *Clitocybe*

13*   Plants thin fleshed, delicate; caps often translucent, striate and hygrophanous; on wood or soil   *14*

14   On soil, often amongst moss; very small and delicate; cap diameter up to 1 cm; umbilicate and striate   *Omphalina*

14*   On wood; umbilicate and striate; sometimes in troops; very similar to the genus *Omphalina* but with a tougher texture and with rather wiry, horny stems   *Xeromphalina*

14**   On wood; cap diameter up to 4 cm; stipes often long and the plants forming caespitose clusters   *Clitocybula*

15   Cap brown to blackish; viscid; stipe long, twisted, rooting and extending into the soil for at least 2 to 5 cm; always on buried wood; usually solitary; (spores smooth, iodine negative)   *Oudemansiella*

15*   Plants not with the above combination of characters; if a rooting structure exists, then plants caespitose   *16*

16   Caps usually conical and at first closely adpressed along the stem, expanding to conical, convex or plane but always with traces of the original pointed state; plants usually delicate; always on or associated with wood; usually clustered or caespitose, but may be in troops; caps thin, often translucent, striate, frequently viscid; gills ascending to adnate; stipe often long, thin and delicate; a reddish fluid may ooze from the stem on cutting   *Mycena*

16*   Plants without the above combination of characters   *17*

17   Plants more or less tough; if dried and then re-moistened, they will recommence to shed spores; on dead wood or plant debris; sometimes forming fairy rings on soil   *Marasmius*

17*   Plants soft; not reviving as above; on or near wood or plant debris (if on soil and flesh or violet tints see *Laccaria*)   *Collybia*

Pink to salmon brown spored genera of the Agaricaceae

18   Volva only present   *Volvaria*

18* No ring or volva present   *19*

19   Gills free; stipe easily removed from cap; always on or near dead wood; (spores smooth)   *Pluteus*

19* Gills adnate, ascending, sinuate or decurrent; (spores polygonal)   *Entoloma*

(NOTE: Some species of *Lepista* may key out here, e.g. those with salmon brown spores and sinuate gills. They are usually very robust plants while the majority of the genus *Entoloma* are relatively small; the critical test is that members of the genus *Lepista* have punctate or prickly spores, while those of *Entoloma* are polygonal.)

Green spored genera of the Agaricaceae

20   One common species only; broadly conical to convex cap with circles of darker scales on the surface; very similar to the genus *Lepiota* but with olive green gills   *Chlorophyllum molybdites*

Rusty to ochre brown spored genera of the Agaricaceae

21   Gills easily removed from the cap by rubbing, often fused together to form large elongated pores, decurrent; the cap generally more or less infundibuliform   *Paxillus*

21* Gills not easily removed from the cap without severely damaging its structure; often forking or 'Y' shaped near the cap margins; may form elongated pores near the stem; cap infundibuliform   *Phylloporus*

21**Not infundibuliform or with branching or fusing gills   *22*

22   Stipe lateral or lacking   *Crepidotus*

22* Stipe central   *23*

23   Cortina present (check very young plants); always on soil; often viscid; sometimes brightly coloured   *Cortinarius*

23* Cortina present, or a *very* thin veil; always on wood and never slimy; plants sometimes caespitose, often with a distinct bitter taste   *Gymnopilus*

23**No cortina present   *24*

24   Ring present; (spores smooth; if rough and the plants growing in troops,

	see *Descolea recedens*)	*Pholiota*
24*	Ring absent	*25*
25	Gills sinuate; plants sturdy, often viscid; amongst or near exotic trees, especially *Pinus spp.* (spores punctate)	*Hebeloma*
25*	Gills not sinuate	*26*
26	Plants fragile; cap conical to campanulate; gills ascending to adnate at the summit; never slimy or viscid; stipe usually long and slender; on lawns; (spores smooth, with germpore; cap cuticle cellular)	*Conocybe*
26*	Plants not as above; if bell-shaped then quite viscid when young and usually a tint or shade of yellow	*27*
27	Very fragile and viscid; usually some shade of yellow when first emerging, the cap eventually liquifying to a more or less gelatinous mess; on very rich soil, manure or heavily fertilised lawns	*Bolbitius*
27*	Plants not with the above set of characters	*28*
28	Cap fibrillose; strongly umbonate; on soil; (spores often nodulose or punctate, large cystidia present on the gills)	*Inocybe*
28*	Cap smooth; hemispherical to convex; (spores punctate)	*Naucoria*

Chocolate-brown spored genera of the Agaricaceae

29	Always with an annulus, no volva; always on soil; in woods or fields; (spores smooth, with or without germ pore)	*Agaricus*

Purple to black spored genera of the Agaricaceae

30	Caps liquefying to an inky-black mess, or the gills auto-digesting and leaving the cap thin and papery; often on very rich soil or dung	*Coprinus*
30*	Caps or gills not liquefying	*31*
31	Spores maturing irregularly so that the gills appear mottled (choose young specimens to see this); on dung	*Panaeolus*
31*	Gills not becoming mottled	*32*
32	Fresh spore print with a tint of purple or violet	*33*
32*	Fresh spore print *pure* black	*34*
33	Gills sinuate; often on wood (which may	

be buried) and usually clustered; generally
bitter tasting   *Hypholoma*

33* Gills adnate to adnexed; on soil or dung;
often with stems which stain blue at the
base if bruised   *Psilocybe*

34 Stipe with a definite ring; on dung or rich
soil; (there are one or two species often
put into the genus *Panaeolus* which may
key out here: the presence of a ring
and/or chrysocystidia confirms the
genus *Stropharia*)   *Stropharia*

34* No ring present   35

35 Stipe and cap strongly fibrillose; gills
weeping in wet weather (spores
very rough)   *Lacrymaria*

35* Stipe and cap smooth; plants generally
rather fragile (spores smooth and
with a germ pore)   *Psathyrella*

THE BOLETACEAE
AND OTHER GENERA

36 Fungus rather like a poached egg or white
meringue, sometimes with purplish or violet
patches where the spores are exposed; on
grass or other vegetable matter, generally
with a small white trail behind it   *Fuligo septica*

36* Fungus like an elongated drumstick, the
head containing a brownish black, powdery
spore mass; stem tough and woody, the head
rather shaggy on the exterior; in dry areas   *Podaxis*

36** Fungus texture distinctly gelatinous, often
more or less translucent; shape coralloid,
brain-like, ear-shaped, a cap with soft spines
or like small gelatinous blobs   *44*

36*** Fungus does not fit into any of the
above sections   *37*

37 Fungus a cap with pores on the under-surface;
a stem may or may not be present   *46*

37* Fungus a cap without pores, or fungus not
a cap-like structure; the puff-balls,
coral-fungi, cup-fungi, etc. fit here   *38*

38 Fungus more or less globular or sack-like;
a buried stem or star shaped base may be

present; spore mass becoming dry and
dusty or the plant simply rotting to release
the spore mass, but the spore mass is
never slimy and foetid on maturity   *55*

38* Fungus does not resemble a ball or sack
on maturity; or spores form a slimy, foetid
smelling mass on maturity   *39*

39   Fungus a cap or bracket structure; smooth
or spiny on the under-surface   *61*

39* Fungus not a cap or bracket structure   *40*

40   Mature spore mass slimy and foul or foetid,
smelling rather like rotten meat or faeces
and attractive to flies; plants usually soft and
spongy and may be star-shaped, phallus shaped
(in which case a lacy veil may be present), like
a lattice work ball, or in the form of a stem with
arms or a lattice-work at the top   *69*

40* Spore mass, if present, not slimy
and foetid at maturity   *41*

41   Fungus coralloid, never gelatinous;
may resemble coral, stag's antlers,
contorted fingers, a club or a spike   *64*

41* Fungus not coralloid or shaped in any
way like the above   *42*

42   Fungus resembles a disc or a cup, with
or without a stalk; on wood, soil, leaf litter
or dung   *73*

42* Not as above   *43*

43   Fungus a fleshy, hollow stem with a
wrinkled, convoluted or pitted head; on soil *Morchella*

43* Fungus a small, top shaped body with
minute, black openings in the flattened
top; always on dung   *Poronia*

44   Fungus a more or less bracket shape or
fan shaped; conical spine shaped
projections on the under-surface;
usually grey, always gelatinous; on wood   *Tremellodon*

44* Fungus more or less coralloid, yellowish
to orange, viscid; a simple spike or
branching; often less than 0.5 cm high   *Calocera*

44** Plant not as above   *45*

45   Fungus a contorted, moist, gelatinous,
translucent, brain-like mass about 3 to
4 cm diameter, sometimes more; orange

to yellow to almost white; always on wood   *Tremella*

45*   Fungus resembles a contorted ear or cup; velvety brown or hairy on the exterior; pinkish brown to pallid brown on the interior; always on wood   *Auricularia*

45** Fungus appears as small, orange-yellow blobs; moist, gelatinous, translucent; always on wood   *Dacrymyces*

46   Stem central   *47*

46*   Stem distinctly lateral or no stem present   *51*

47   Cap surface with large shaggy scales like a pine-cone; always on wood (spores fusiform, longitudinally striate — if spores more or less globose and decorated with a raised network, see *Strobilomyces spp.*)   *Boletellus*

47*   Cap smooth, viscid, or with closely adpressed scales, but never resembling a pine-cone in roughness   *48*

48   Pores purple; plants orange and very viscid on both the cap and stem; flesh very soft and juicy   *Austroboletus*

48*   Not as above   *49*

49   Pores easily removable from cap; flesh thick; often under introduced trees   *Boletus*

49*   Pores very difficult or impossible to remove without severely damaging the plant   *50*

50   Pores about 2 mm or more in diameter; hexagonal or at least polygonal, and radially arranged   *Favolus*

50*   Pores much smaller and round (if pores stain red, see *Amauroderma sp.*)   *Polyporus*

51   Plant looks and feels like a large tongue or a piece of liver; pores are separate on maturity   *Fistulina*

51*   Plant not as above   *52*

52   Pores minute, about five per millimetre, and must be observed with a hand lens; caps thin, stipes lateral   *Microporus*

52*   Pores generally much larger, but usually no lateral stipe present; cap affixed directly onto the wood substrate   *53*

53   Pores in several layers; plants very hard and woody   *Fomes*

53*   Pores form a maze like a labyrinth   *Daedalea*

53**Plants not as above   *54*

54   A transverse cut reveals that the single
      layer of pores has tubes that run at different
      levels into the cap flesh.
      a) brackets brilliant red orange   *Pycnoporus*
      b) brackets lilac or zoned light-dark   *Trametes*

54*   All the pores are at the same depth in the
      cap flesh, which is usually over 1 cm thick
      and is soft in consistency, sometimes juicy   *Polyporus*

55   Fungus has its ball or sack on a star-like base   *56*

55*   No such star-shaped base present   *57*

56   Sack or peridium has a single opening   *Geastrum*

56*   Sack has several to many openings   *Myriostoma*

57   A transverse section reveals the gleba is
      divided into many tiny compartments each
      about the size of a rice grain; a long stipe
      may be present; the upper portion of the
      peridium slowly crumbles away to release
      the rusty yellow or purplish brown
      spore mass   *Pisolithus*

57*   No such compartments present, or only
      found in very immature plants, and if this
      is so then the spores are not released by the
      slow crumbling away of the peridium   *58*

58   Spore mass never becoming dry and dusty,
      the fungus simply rotting to release the
      spores; fungus is a hard, solid ball or oval
      and may have white rhizomorphs attached;
      sometimes turning pink on bruising;
      half-buried in soil, frequently under
      introduced species of pines   *Rhizopogon*

58*   Spore mass becoming dry and dusty;
      fungus either splitting open, or the walls
      of the peridium disintegrating to about
      halfway down their sides to produce a
      wide ragged opening   *59*

58**Spore mass becoming dry and dusty, but
      released through a definite opening at the
      top of the peridium   60

59   Fungus splits open at maturity; peridial
      walls thick like a rind   *Scleroderma*

59*   Fungus with a peridium which becomes
      thin and papery at maturity, the walls

| | disintegrating from the summit down and releasing the dry, dusty spore mass | *Calvatia* |

60 Fungus attached to a short, underground stem about 2 to 3 cm long and about 2 to 3 mm diameter *Tulostoma*

60* No such underground stem *Lycoperdon*

61 Fungus infundibuliform, thin fleshed; smooth on the funnel under-surface *Craterellus*

61* Not as above *62*

62 Fungus with spines under the cap *Hydnum*

62* Fungus smooth under the cap *63*

63 Cap thin and bracket-like; hairy or smooth on the upper surface; on wood; margin undulating but even; (spores smooth, hyaline, no iodine reaction) *Stereum*

63* Cap thin, often forming rosettes; shaggy, uneven; on soil surface or pine needles, plant debris or wood; one species is common in woods of introduced pines (spores rough, spiny, lobed and brownish) *Thelephora*

64 Coralloid; each branch ends in a tiny cup, from the rim of which then spring other branches and the process continues, each branch getting smaller; always on wood *Clavicorona*

64* Not forming small cups with branches from the rims *65*

65 On wood; texture very firm; may resemble contorted fingers, clubs or tiny antlers; a hand lens reveals that the surface is covered with tiny holes or pimples *Xylaria*

65* On soil; club-shaped; pure black; velvety *Trichoglossum*

65** On wood or soil; never pure black, and often brightly coloured; soft in texture *66*

66 On soil; excavation reveals that the plant springs from the mummified body of a caterpillar or pupa; plant structure like a club or stag's antlers; a hand lens reveals tiny holes or pimples *Cordyceps*

66* Not as above *67*

67 On soil; forms dense coralline masses which may be up to 20 cm in diameter; very branched with thick stems at the base; colour frequently ochre, purple, salmon,

yellow or pink; (spores ochre, spiny
or rough)   *Ramaria*

67* On soil, plant debris, moss or very rotten
     wood, but always rather fragile and
     delicate; often very branched, but never
     forming large masses as with the
     Ramaria spp.   68

68   Fungus branched or simple; circular in
     cross-section   *Clavaria*

68* Fungus simple to scarcely branched;   *Clavulinopsis*
     bright red; flattened in cross-section;   *miniata*
     sometimes contorted

69   Fungus more or less phallus-like; stipe
     about 8 to 16 cm long, and there may be a
     veil hanging from the top cap which is
     covered with a greenish olive, foetid slime   70

69* Not as above   71

70   Fungus with a lacy veil hanging down from
     the top; the veil may be pure white or
     brightly coloured   *Dictyophora*

70* No veil present   *Phallus*

71   Fungus a more or less spherical lattice
     with the spore mass on the inside; a short
     stem may be present; plants may be
     brightly coloured, red, green or white   *Clathrus*

71* Fungus a stem with arms or finger-like
     appendages; these may meet at the top to
     form a small network or lattice, but only
     at the extreme top   72

72   Upper portion a star with bright red arms;
     the arms in pairs radiating from a central
     disc on which the olive, slimy, foetid spore
     mass is placed (a white variety exists)   *Aseroe*

72* Upper portion of the stem is divided into
     five to seven arms which are free from
     each other and which project vertically
     upwards; the spore mass is on the inner
     surfaces of the arms   *Lysurus*

72** Practically no stem is present; about three
     or four arms project upwards and are
     joined by a few strands at their extreme
     ends   *Anthurus*

72***Practically no stem present; about five
     to seven arms project vertically upwards

and join to form a small lattice work at their
extreme ends; bright red   *Colus*

73 Tiny, green, stalked discs up to 5 mm
    diameter; on dead wood which becomes
    stained green   *Chlorosplenium*

73* Discs or cups of various colours, sometimes
    more or less flattened and contorted; on
    manure or soil (if disc has minute black
    holes in its upper surface, see 43)   *74*

74 Small cups to little more than 5 mm
    diameter; at first closed by a membrane;
    inside the cups are small, flattened,
    bean shaped objects; on manure, sticks
    or vegetable debris   *75*

74* More or less fleshy discs or cups, often
    brightly coloured but never with small,
    flattened, bean shaped objects inside   *77*

75 On manure   *Cyathus
                                             stercoreus*

75* On sticks, plant debris   *76*

76 White to cream; exterior rather
    shaggy tomentose   *Nidula*

76* Cinnamon brown and silkysmooth on
    the exterior   *Crucibulum*

77 Large, black, rubbery-textured, stemmed
    cups 2 to 3 cm diameter; always on
    dead wood   *Plectania*

77* Small, reddish cups or discs, fringed with
    short, blackish hairs; always on manure *Cheilymenia*

77**Discs, cups or contorted discs; often
    brightly coloured in reds or yellows; on soil   *Peziza*

SPECIES DESCRIPTIONS

Notes on the Descriptions

1. Throughout this work, some species described may be found to be close to, but not identical with, already well-known and described species. In these cases, the author has used the convention of including the abbreviation 'aff.', indicating that the Australian plant has not yet been named and has an affinity with an already published and named species but is not necessarily identical to it.

2   Dimensions are given in micrometres (μm). Cross-sections or habit sketches are not to scale, but dimensions are given in the text; relative dimensions of the parts of a section or habit sketch are correct.

3   Where a species has not been collected by the author, and a previously published description has been referred to, this is so acknowledged in the text.

4   Within the fungal orders described herein, genera and species have, for convenience, been placed in alphabetical order rather than a strict taxonomical arrangement.

5   Where modern taxonomic concepts have caused changes in the genus to which a species is assigned by this volume, the preferred genus is indicated in the text. (This is particularly so for the polyporoid genera.) In most cases, the older name has been used by this work to permit ready and simple usage of the keys.

BASIDIOMYCOTINA

TREMELLALES

Tremella mesenterica Retz. ex Hook.

Forms highly contorted, convoluted masses suggestive of a brain or intestines up to 10 cm diameter; pallid yellow to bright orange; growing directly on the substrate; moistly gelatinous and translucent.

SMELL None.

SPORES 13–14 x 7–8 μm; white, hyaline under the microscope; smooth; basidia tetra-spored.

HABITAT On dead wood; often gregarious.

QLD NSW VIC SA WA

Tremella fuciformis Berk. is similar but pure white. Recorded from rainforests in Queensland.

Tremellodon gelatinosum (Scop.:Fr.) Fr.

CAP Grey-white to brownish; to 5 cm diameter; attached directly to the substrate or on a short, lateral stem; gelatinous, translucent; surface smooth or wrinkled.

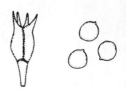

SPINES Greyish to dusty white; up to 4 mm long; more or less conical.

SPORES 4–7 μm; sub-globose; hyaline; smooth; apiculus prominent.

HABITAT Solitary on dead wood or bark.

NSW QLD

AURICULARIALES

Auricularia aff. *auricula-judae* Fr.

CAP Rusty, tawny brown to sepia above, pale clay-pink to whitish below;

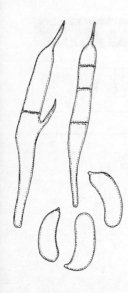

shell-shaped or like a contorted ear; upper surface very finely velvety, but not hairy, lower surface smooth and wrinkled; tissues gelatinous and sometimes a little translucent; may be a little rubbery; drying horny.

SMELL None TASTE Mild. Edible

SPORES 12.5–13 x 5–5.5 μm; hyaline; curved; apiculus prominent; basidia septate.

HABITAT Gregarious on wood.

QLD NSW

NOTE This species is common in the rain forests and wet sclerophyll forests of southern Queensland. *A. polytricha* (Montagne) Sacc. has a dense coating of fine short hairs on the cap upper surface; this last species also occurs in NSW and QLD.

DACRYMYCETALES

Calocera sinensis McNabb

Forms tiny, finger-like spikes which are simple or occasionally dichotomous at the top; up to 2 cm high, 1 to 1.5 mm thick; flat; usually acuminate, occasionally rounded. Bright yellow to orange; moist; gelatinous, a little viscid.

SPORES 9.5–10.5 x 4.5–5.5 μm ; hyaline, smooth; curved with a prominent apiculus; uni-septate; no iodine reaction. Very small, smooth, hyaline, oblong conidiospores, (4 x 1.5), are often present.

HABITAT Gregarious on rotting wood.

WA SA VIC NSW QLD

Dacrymyces stillatus Nees : Fr.

Very variable, but usually pustular and resembling gelatinous blobs up to 2 cm diameter, generally smaller; yellow to

orange-yellow; hyphae lack clamp con-
nections.

SPORES 13–16 x 4.5–5.5 μm ; elliptic to
slightly curved; tri-septate; smooth;
hyaline; basidia bispored.

HABITAT Dead wood or fallen branches.

SA

APHYLLOPHORALES

Polyporaceae

Amauroderma rude (Berk.) Cunn.[= *Polyporus rudis* Berk.]

CAP To 8 cm; zoned light and dark
brown; convex, flattened or umbilicate; rough or smooth, often with
grass or twigs embedded; dry; faintly velvety.

FLESH Creamy-brown; turns red on
cutting.

PORES White to greyish, 3 per mm;
turn red immediately on bruising.

STEM To 13 cm, snuff-brown; smooth
to knobbly; central to slightly excentric often distorted.

SPORES 7–10 x 6–8 μm; golden yellow; ellipsoid; faintly punctate or
verrucose.

SMELL None.

HABITAT On very rotten logs, stumps or
buried wood; sometimes gregarious.

TAS QLD NSW VIC

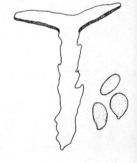

Favolus arcularius (Fr.) Ames [=*Polyporus arcularius* (Bat.) Fr.]

CAP To 5 cm; ochraceous with
brownish, closely adpressed scales;
more or less umbilicate, often with
fine hairs at margin.

FLESH White, thin, tough; no colour
change in potassium hydroxide;
clamps present.

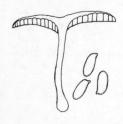

PORES More or less polygonal; about 2 mm diameter with finely ragged edges; light brown.
STEM To 6 cm; creamy brown and appearing coated with minute, adpressed, brownish granules.
SPORES 8 x 3 μm; hyaline; oblong; smooth.
SMELL None.
HABITAT On dead wood (which may be buried), often gregarious.
WA NSW QLD

Fistulina hepatica (Huds.) Fr.

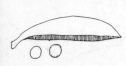

To 10 cm; reddish brown to dark brown; viscid; papillate; radially wrinkled.
FLESH Brownish to red-brown; fibrous.
PORES Bright flesh-pink; stippled red; separate from each other on maturity.
STEM Lateral; short or lacking; concolorous with cap.
SPORES 5 x 3.5 μm; hyaline; smooth.
SMELL None. **TASTE** Mild to acidic. Edible.
HABITAT Solitary on dead eucalypt wood
NSW VIC SA WA QLD

Microporus flabelliformis (Klotz.) Kuntze

CAP To 5 cm; clay-pink becoming vinaceous-brown; fan-shaped; smooth; dry; rubbery in appearance; edge even, slightly inrolled.
FLESH Whitish cream; clamps present; no change in KOH.
PORES Minute; round; white becoming creamy yellow; 10 to 12 per mm.
STEM To 3 cm; sepia; lateral; velvety.
SPORES 3.5–4 x 1.5–2 μm; hyaline; smooth; elliptical or cylindrical.
SMELL Musty.
HABITAT Solitary on dead wood.
NSW QLD VIC

Polyporus australiensis Wakefield [=Piptoporus australiensis (Wakefield) Cunn.]

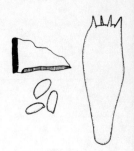

CAP to 25cm; dirty creamy white, often discoloured yellow; convex; dry; smooth

flesh Creamy white; thick; exuding a saffron juice which is very staining.

PORES Bright orange; may weep saffron juice.

SPORES 8–9 x 5–6μm; hyaline; oblong; smooth.

SMELL Pungent, musty, of curry.

HABITAT On dead wood, usually recently fire-charred.

WA SA VIC NSW QLD TAS The juice is excellent for dyeing

Polyporus oblectans Berk. [= *Coltricia oblectans* (Berk.) Cunn.]

CAP To 2.5 cm; brown and zoned with paler areas; satiny sheen; radially fibrillose; infundibuliform, the centre with a small tuft of hairs; paler at the margin.

FLESH Concolorous with cap; very thin.

PORES Pale lilac; irregularly polygonal; edges minutely villose; decurrent.

STEM To 2 cm; tough; solid; dusty clay-brown.

SPORES 6–8 x 4–5 μm; yellowish; broadly elliptical.

SMELL None.

HABITAT Gregarious on soil amongst litter, often at the bases of old stumps.

WA NT QLD NSW VIC TAS SA

Polyporus pelliculosis Berk. [= *Tyromyces pelliculosis* (Berk.) Cunn.]

CAP 10 cm; brown; strigose; fan-shaped.

FLESH Faint salmon-pink; thick.

PORES Pallid, or faintly pink or lilac;

turn brown when bruised.

SPORES 4.5–5.5 x 3.5–4.5 μm; whitish; elliptical; smooth; apiculus prominent.

HABITAT At the bases of living trees.

WA SA VIC NSW TAS

Polyporus portentosus Berk.
[=*Piptoporus portentosus* (Berk.) Cunn.]

CAP To 30 cm; cream to smoky brown; up to 12 cm thick; smooth; dry.

FLESH Pure white; soft; thick; pithy.

PORES Straw yellow becoming greyish.

SPORES 8–10 x 6–8.5 μm; white; sub-globose; smooth.

HABITAT High on the trunks of living trees, especially eucalypts; solitary; parasitic, reducing the heart-wood to sheets of papery material; sporophore soon insect-riddled and falling from the tree.

WA SA VIC NSW TAS QLD

Polyporus tumulosus Cke. & Mass.

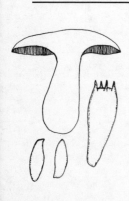

CAP To 16 cm; buff to brownish; dry; convex but with wavy or even up-turned margins; cuticle cracking to expose the white flesh beneath.

FLESH White, thick.

PORES Creamy; discoloured brown in spots.

STEM To 6 cm; blackish; thick; stout; extends down to a large, false scle-rotium which may be a metre under-ground.

SPORES 10–15 x 5–6 μm; white; fusi-form smooth.

SMELL Unpleasant, burnt odour.

HABITAT Amongst ashes around stumps after trees have been felled, or around stumps after a forest fire; appears to need the stimulus of a fire before it will produce a sporophore.

WA SA VIC TAS NSW QLD

Pycnoporus coccineus (Fr.) Bondarzew & Singer

CAP To 6 cm; orange-red to vermillion, fading to pinkish white; smooth; fan-shaped.

FLESH Creamy white; coriaceous; thick.

PORES Brilliant vermillion; circular; very small.

SPORES 5 x 2.5 μm; white; cylindrical or slightly curved; smooth; no iodine reaction; basidia 4-spored

SMELL None or musty.

Stereum hirsutum (Willd. : Fr.) S.F. Gray

CAP To 8 cm; zoned with light and dark orange-brown, darkest at the attachment point; hispid or shortly hirsute; wavy, lobed, irregularly folded.

FLESH Whitish yellow; thin; coriaceous.

HYMENIUM Smooth; yellow-brown to orange.

SPORES 6–8 x 3–4 μm; hyaline; smooth; cylindrical; no iodine reaction.

SMELL None.

HABITAT Solitary or gregarious in tiers or single brackets on dead wood.

WA SA QLD

Stereum illudens Berk.

CAP To 7 cm; deep brown, paler at the margin; zoned; strigose; undulating or lobed.

FLESH Concolorous with cap, very thin; coriaceous.

HYMENIUM Sepia; zoned; orange tints at the margin; acutely tipped cystidia present; often appearing dusty.

SPORES 9 x 4 μm; cylindrical; smooth; hyaline; no iodine reaction; basidia 4-spored.

SMELL None.

HABITAT In tiers on dead wood.

SA NSW

HABITAT Gregarious on any dead wood.

QLD NSW VIC TAS SA WA

Trametes lilacino-gilva (Berk.) Lloyd

CAP To 5 cm; brown, tinted lilac to violet; irregularly convex; smooth.
FLESH Rosy lilac to lilac; firm; corky; thick.
PORES Lilac; round; 4 to 5 per mm; there is a 1 to 2 mm non-pored area around the cap margin.

SPORES 6–9 x 2.5–3 μm; hyaline;
SMELL Musty.
HABITAT Dead wood

WA SA VIC TAS NSW QLD NT

Trametes versicolor (L. : Fr.) Pil.

CAP To 6 cm; 2 to 5 mm thick; zoned with light and dark bands; colour varies from yellow to orange to brown or most commonly bluish black; margin always lighter; smooth to strigose.
FLESH White; thin; coriaceous.
PORES White to off-white; 3 to 5 per mm.
SPORES 4–6 x 1.5–2 μm; white; elliptical smooth; basidia 4 spored.
SMELL None.
HABITAT Gregarious on old dead stumps or fallen logs; often in spectacular tiered arrangements; very common.

TAS QLD NSW VIC SA WA NT

NOTE Other generic names for this species have been *Polyporus, Coriolus* and *Polystictus*; the specific name of *versicolor* has rarely been challenged. Two close relatives are possibly subvarieties. *T. zonata* has an orange-brown cap in which the zones are alternately strigose and smooth; *T. azurea* is deep blue to lilac with distinctly yellow pores.

HYDNACEAE

Hydnum crocidens Cooke

CAP To 4 cm; creamy white, bruising brown or yellowish orange; irregularly convex to plane or repand.

FLESH White; brittle; stains bright saffron to ochre.

SPINES Creamy brown or concolorous with cap; up to 5 mm long; adnate to decurrent.

STEM To 5 cm; whitish to creamy, staining brownish; slender; central or a little excentric.

SPORES 7–8.5 μm; white; smooth; globose.

SMELL None. **TASTE** Mild to bitter.

HABITAT Solitary or gregarious on soil in woods amongst leaf mould.

NSW SA QLD WA

THELEPHORACEAE

Thelephora terrestris Ehrh. : Fr.

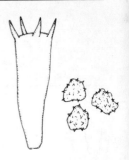

CAP To 10 cm; sepia to rusty brown; forming brackets, rosettes or irregular, matted cap-like surfaces amongst plant debris; upper surface hairy; margins ragged, torn or lobed; hymenium smooth, light violet-brown to rusty brown, appearing dusty.

SPORES 10–11 x 7–8 μm; pallid rusty brown; globular, but lobed and spiny or warted; basidia 4-spored.

HABITAT On soil or needles under exotic pines, especially *Pinus spp.*

WA SA NSW VIC

CLAVARIACEAE

Clavaria acuta Fr.

SPOROPHORE To 8 cm; pure white;

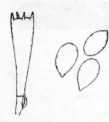

unbranched; cylindrical; acutely tipped; brittle; hollow..

SPORES 7–10 x 5–9 μm; white; smooth; ellipsoid to globose; basidia 2 or 4-spored.

SMELL None. TASTE None.

HABITAT Solitary or gregarious amongst grass or litter in fields or woods.

VIC NSW

Clavaria amethystina Fr. [=*Clavulina amethystina* (Fr.) Donk]

The shift from *Clavaria* to *Clavulina* Schroet. is because the very distinctive basidia have two, curved sterigmata. It is possible that the species in Australia may only be close to the European species, and not the same.)

SPOROPHORE To 8 cm; amythyst, violet, lilac or pinkish lilac, the tips often darker, esp. with age; branching to only sparingly so; brittle; flesh concolorous; axils rounded; tips acute.

SPORES 7–8 x 6–7 μm; white; smooth; sub-globuse; basidia 2-spored.

SMELL None. TASTE None.

HABITAT On soil, under trees or shrubs.

WA SA VIC

Clavulinopsis miniata (Berk.) Corner

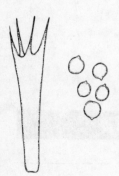

COMMON NAME Flame Fungus

SPOROPHORE To 10 cm; orange-pink to flame orange or reddish orange; sometimes a little yellow at the tips; may be whitish at the base; simple or shortly branched; often flattened in cross-section, and may be fan-shaped; longitudinally grooved; slightly tough, becoming hollow; may curl over and become distorted; surface may be punctate with black dots.

SPORES 5–7 x 4.5–6.5 μm; white; smooth; globose with a short apiculus; basidia 2, 3 or 4-spored, but mostly

4-spored.

SMELL None. **TASTE** None.

HABITAT On soil amongst litter; rarely solitary, gregarious to caespitose.

VIC NSW

Clavicorona pyxidata (Fr.) Doty

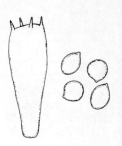

SPOROPHORE To 12 cm; yellowish, dull ochre, tan to light brown; occasionally whitish or pinkish; each branch terminates in a small cup, from the rim of which arise 4 to 6 new, smaller branches and so on up to the terminal tips; base whitish or pinkish; surface smooth

SPORES 4–5 x 2–3 μm; white; elliptical; smooth; basidia 4-spored.

SMELL None. **TASTE** Mild to peppery.

HABITAT On dead wood; caespitose to gregarious.

NSW VIC

Ramaria fumigata (Pk.) Corner

SPOROPHORE To 12 cm; violet or purplish but sooty-brown with age, the tips remaining purple; extremely branched, crowded and compact; flesh white or creamy; *may* bruise reddish.

SPORES 8.5–12.5 x 4–5.5 μm; ochre brown; elliptical; rough to almost smooth; a large central globule to present; basidia 4-spored.

SMELL None. **TASTE** None.

HABITAT In dense clumps on soil amongst leaf litter.

QLD VIC SA

Ramaria ochraceo-salmonicolor [(Clel.) Corner]

SPOROPHORE To 14 cm; light yellow and all shades to pinkish orange; very branched but tightly clustered so that the plant resembles a cauliflower; ultimate tips rounded.

SPORES 8–10.5 x 4–5.5 μm; ochre

brown; elliptical; rough.

HABITAT In large clumps on soil amongst forest floor litter.

VIC SA NSW QLD

Ramaria sinapicolor (Clel.) Corner

SPOROPHORE To 12 cm; light yellow to orange yellow but yellowish towards the tips; stems slender, branching and densely collected into a main trunk; flesh white or creamy; axils rounded.

SPORES 6–10 x 3–4.5 μm; ochre; elliptical; rough.

SMELL Sweet. **TASTE** Mild. Edible.

HABITAT In dense caespitose clumps on soil amongst forest litter; possibly mycorrhizal with eucalypts.

NSW VIC SA WA

NOTE See also the species *R. subaurantiaca* with which the above species may be confused.

Ramaria subaurantiaca Corner

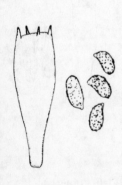

SPOROPHORE To 10 cm; salmon orange; base white; densely branched; axils rounded; ultimate tips bluntly rounded; flesh white, brittle.

SPORES 7–8.5 x 3.5–4.5 μm; ochre; elliptical; rough.

SMELL None. **TASTE** Mild.

HABITAT On sandy soil in dense clumps amongst woodland litter.

NSW QLD

NOTE This species may be confused with the species *R. sinapicolor* however *R. sinapicolor* always has a distinct tint of yellow, whilst *R. sub-aurantiaca* is a distinct pinkish orange to salmond pink.

CANTHARELLACEAE

Cantharellus concinnus Berk

CAP To 3 cm; apricot gold or orange; smooth; dry infundibuliform; scalloped at the margin.

FLESH Concolorous with cap; thin.

GILLS Pale apricot; decurrent; distant; often forking near the margin and tending to be gill-like ridges rather than true gills.

STEM To 2 cm; concolorous with the cap; thinner towards the base; smooth; no ring or volva.

SPORES 6.5–9 x 5–7 μm; white; oval; smooth; basidia 4-spored.

SMELL None or faintly of apricots.

TASTE None or mild to peppery. Edible.

HABITAT Gregarious on soil amongst forest litter.

NSW VIC

Cantharellus pusio Berk. [= *Podoserpula pusio* (Berk.) Reid = *Craterellus multiplex* Cke. & Mass.]

CAP To 3 cm; white to yellowish or light brown; irregularly kidney-shaped and infundibuliform; either solitary or up to 6 caps superimposed in tiers on a common lateral stem, with each cap becoming progressively smaller; smooth; dry; margins slightly incurved.

FLESH Whitish; very thin.

GILLS Vinaceous-pink; almost non-existent or reduced to a series of blunt ridges or the surface simply rather tubercular.

STEM To 5 cm; pale brown; dry; more or less lateral; no ring or volva.

SPORES 4 x 3.5 μm; white; globose; smooth.

HABITAT Solitary or gregarious on

soil at the base of very old rotting stumps.

VIC TAS SA NSW WA

Craterellus cornucopioides Pers.

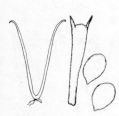

CAP To 12 cm; dark brown to black-ish; infundibuliform; margins wavy, lobed or splitting; cuticle rather scaly.
FLESH Thin; tough.
HYMENIUM Whitish to greyish; smooth.
SPORES 12–15 x 7–9 μm; white; smooth; oval; no iodine reaction; basidia 2 or 4-spored.
HABITAT Caespitose or gregarious amongst tree litter on soil.

QLD NSW VIC

AGARICALES

AGARICACEAE

Agaricus arvensis Schaeff. ex Secr. sensu Lange

COMMON NAME Horse Mushroom.
CAP To 15 cm; white to brownish; yellowish with age; spherical becoming convex, then plane; cuticle dry, peeling; smooth or with a few scales; often with veil remnants at the margin.
FLESH Thick, white; yellowish where cut especially in the stem.
GILLS Pallid becoming pink then chocolate brown; free; crowded.
STEM To 10 cm; white; yellowish with age; hollow; smooth; no volva; ring white, fixed, two-layered, the upper layer pendulous, the lower toothed like a cog-wheel.
SPORES 7.5 x 4.5 μm; oval; smooth; chocolate brown; basidia 4-spored.
SMELL Pleasant, of aniseed.

TASTE Pleasant. Edible.

HABITAT Gregarious in pastures; often in fairy rings.

QLD NSW VIC SA

Agaricus bisporus (Lange) Pilat.

COMMON NAME Cultivated Mushroom.

CAP To 7 cm; pallid to brown; convex to plane; smooth to fibrillosely scaly; margin inrolled with veil fragments.

FLESH White, reddening or browning a little on exposure to air; thick.

GILLS Pink becoming chocolate brown; edges pallid and uneven; free; crowded.

STEM To 5 cm; grey-white; slightly bulbous at the base; flesh reddens on cutting; ring fixed, white, membranous; stem easily detached from cap.

SPORES 6.5–8 x 5–6 μm; chocolate brown; oval; smooth; basidia 2-spored.

SMELL Faintly aromatic. TASTE Mild. Edible and fairly good.

HABITAT On soil under shrubs.

AUSTRALIA Generally.

Agaricus campestris L : Fr. sensu Lange

COMMON NAME Field Mushroom.

CAP To 10 cm; pure white, but sometimes a little brown stained or pinkish; globular then convex; margin usually with veil fragments; cuticle smooth, peeling, dry.

FLESH White, pinkish where exposed to the air, especially in the stem; thick.

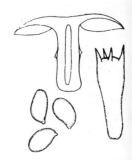

GILLS Bright pink becoming chocolate brown; free; crowded.

STEM To 8 cm; white; solid; easily

detached from cap; ring white, fixed,
thin, friable and easily destroyed; no
volva.

SPORES 7–8 x 4.5–5.5 μm; chocolate
brown; smooth; oval; basindia 4-
spored.

SMELL Pleasant. **TASTE** Pleasant.
Edible and very good.

HABITAT In troops in pastures or
lawns; single or caespitose.

AUSTRALIA Generally.

Agaricus aff. *langei* (Moll.) Moll.

CAP To 10 cm; fawn to wine-brown;
convex to plane; rather fibrillose
with tiny, adpressed scales; cuticle
peeling; margin with occasional veil
remnants.

FLESH White, turning faintly reddish
brown; thin.

GILLS Pallid, then pinky grey, finally
light chocolate brown, often with a
wine red tint; crowded; free.

STEM To 8 cm; white; flocculose
below the ring; solid becoming hollow; easily detached from cap; ring
white, simple and flocculose on the
lower surface; no volva.

SPORES 5.5 x 3.5 μm; chocolate brown;
oval; smooth; basidia 4-spored.

SMELL None. **TASTE** Mild. Edible.

HABITAT Solitary amongst eucalypt
litter on soil of hillsides.

NSW VIC SA WA

Agaricus xanthoderma Genevier
[= *A. arvensis* var. iodoformis Clel. & Cheel]

CAP To 10 cm; white (some variations are brownish and scaly); quickly staining yellow where bruised;
globular then convex; smooth or
with greyish scales, especially at the
centre; cuticle peels.

FLESH White, yellowing when cut; thick.

GILLS Greyish, then grey-pink, finally chocolate-grey; crowded; free.

STEM To 8 cm; white, staining yellow; hollow; flesh at stem base turns yellow instantly on cutting; bulbous at the base; ring fixed, white (but may be yellowish), double; stem easily detached from cap; no volva.

SPORES 5–6.5 x 3–4 μm; grey chocolate brown; smooth; oval; basidia 4-spored.

SMELL Unpleasant, like indian ink or iodine.

TASTE Mild to unpleasant. Edibility suspect; best avoided. Some people eat it with no ill effects, others suffer severe stomach upsets.

HABITAT On soil under shrubs or trees in twos or threes.

QLD VIC NSW SA

Amanita farinacea (Sacc.) Clel. & Cheel.

COMMON NAME Yellow stainer.

CAP To 8 cm; white; globular then convex; a little viscid and covered with white fragments of the universal veil; cuticle peels.

FLESH White; thick.

GILLS White, creamy with age; free; crowded; edges serrate.

STEM To 8 cm; white; base conico-bulbous; flocculose; solid; ring very friable, white, rapidly disappearing; volva white, very friable, rapidly disappearing to leave only a few white fragments at the base.

SPORES 9.5–12 x 6.5–8 μm; white; smooth; amyloid; basidia 4-spored.

SMELL Nitric or like urine, very strong **TASTE** Nauseating.

HABITAT On rich soil amongst

eucalypt forest litter; often gregarious; usually scatters its surroundings with white, fragments of its veils.

NSW VIC SA WA

Amanita muscaria (L. : Fr.) Hooker

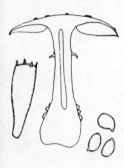

VERY POISONOUS

COMMON NAME Fly Agaric.

CAP To 10 cm; orange-red to scarlet but dotted with white fragments of the universal veil; globular then convex, finally plane; viscid; margin usually striate.

FLESH White but yellowish directly under the cuticle; thick.

GILLS White; edges very finely serrate; crowded; free.

STEM To 10 cm; white; solid; base bulbous; apex striate, remainder often flocculose and the base with a series of rings of white scales; ring white-yellowish, a little striate, pendulous, large.

SPORES 8–10 x 6–7 μm; white; smooth; amyloid; basidia 4-spored.

SMELL None. TASTE Mild to burning. Very poisonous, but rarely lethal.

HABITAT On soil amongst forest litter; usually in association with introduced trees, especially oak, birch and pine.

NSW VIC SA

NOTE First recorded in NSW at Kurrajong Heights under *Pinus sp.* 1980.

Amanita nauseosa (Wakefield) Reid

CAP To 12 cm; convex; ochre brown or orange-brown; more or less shaggy, with the cap edge having abundant, pendulous velar fragments; 'sticky' to the touch, the particles of the universal veil present on the cap readily adhere to the fingers.

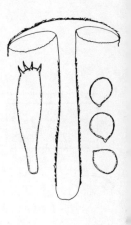

FLESH Ochre brown; turgid; weeps when cut with a clear liquid which may turn orange later.

GILLS Concolorous with cap or slightly paler; crowded; edges more or less serrate.

STEM To 15 (20) cm; 1 to 1.5 cm thick; solid; concolorous with cap; covered with shaggy floccules and velar fragments which also adhere to the fingers on touching.

SPORES 8.0–8.6 (8.9) μm; hyaline; smooth; amyloid; sub-globose; basidia 4-spored.

SMELL Nitric or urinous, nauseating and very strong.

HABITAT In pairs or small groups on soil in sheltered or open places, amongst litter or grass.

WA NSW QLD

NOTE Without careful examination this species may easily be mistaken for a member of the *Lepiota* complex.

Amanita ochrophylla (Cke. & Mass.) Clel.

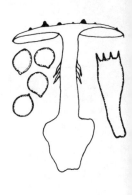

CAP To 15 cm; apricot-buff, then creamy white remaining buff at the centre; convex then plane; surface covered with large pyramidal warts; veil fragments at margin.

FLESH White; thick.

GILLS White to pallid-pink; crowded; free; edge minutely serrate.

STEM To 15 cm; white; solid; base very large, conical, rooting; annulus large, white, fixed pendulous, striate above, floccose below; volva remains as a ring of white, basal fragments.

SPORES 10–11.5 x 9.5 μm; white; smooth; sub-spherical; basidia 4-spored.

SMELL Strong but pleasant.

TASTE Nutty. Edibility unknown.

HABITAT On soil amongst forest litter;
gregarious.

NSW VIC SA

Amanita phalloides (Vaill. : Fr.) Secr.

**VERY
POISONOUS**

COMMON NAME Death Cap.

CAP To 12 cm; olive-brown to yellowish or greenish; spherical then convex, finally plane; slightly viscid;
sometimes with a few volval fragments on the surface.

FLESH White, may be slightly greenish
just below the cap cuticle; thick.

GILLS White; free; close; turn pinkish
lilac if a drop of concentrated sul-
phuric acid is placed on them.

STEM To 10 cm; slightly yellowish to
white; stout; bulbous base; solid;
smooth; ring large, fixed, sheathing,
irregular, white.

SPORES 9–11 x 7–9 μm; white; smooth;
sub-spherical; amyloid; basidia 4-
spored.

SMELL Faintly nauseous. TASTE Mild.
Deadly poisonous.

HABITAT Under introduced trees, esp.
oak.

NSW ACT VIC

Amanita preissii (Fr.) McAlp.

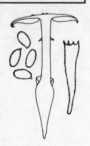

**VERY
POISONOUS**

CAP To 8 cm; white; spherical, then
convex, margin inrolled; a little viscid;
smooth.

FLESH White; thick.

GILLS White; crowded; free.

STEM To 8 cm; white; base conical;
solid; smooth above the ring, mealy
below; ring white, often brown
stained, ragged, pendulous; volva
white, sheathing and persistent.

SPORES 11–12 x 5–6.5 μm; white;
smooth; elliptical; basidia 4-spored.

SMELL A mixture of sweet, sour and oily.

TASTE Not recorded. Poisonous.

HABITAT On sandy soil under shrubs.

WA NSW

Amanita punctata (Clel. & Cheel) Reid. [= *Amanitopsis punctata* Clel & Cheel.]

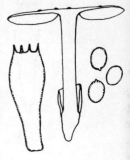

CAP To 8 cm; conical then convex, finally plane; smooth; margin strongly striate.

FLESH White; thin.

GILLS White to slightly greyish; crowded; adnexed.

STEM To 10 cm; grey; cuticle cracking into uneven patches of grey and white; slender; no ring; volva loose, grey, sheathing.

SPORES 11 x 10 μm; white; globose; no iodine reaction; basidia 4-spored.

SMELL None. TASTE Sweetish. Possibly edible; no records for this Australian species; best avoided.

HABITAT On soil amongst forest litter; often solitary, but has been found in small groups.

QLD NSW WA VIC

Amanita xanthocephala (Berk.) Reid & Hilton.

CAP To 5 cm; orange-yellow to pale orange, lighter at the margin; convex then plane; lightly viscid with white patches of the volva; margin striate.

FLESH White; thin.

GILLS White; crowded; free.

STEM To 5 cm; white; thin; no ring; volva small, white, cup-like, edge often bright yellow.

SPORES 7–11 x 8–9 μm; white; smooth; sub-globose with a prominent apiculus; no iodine reaction; basidia 4-spored.

SMELL None. TASTE None.

HABITAT On soil amongst litter under shrubs.

NSW VIC SA WA QLD

Armillaria hinnulea Kile & Watling.

CAP To 8 cm; sepia with traces of olive green and yellow with olive green tints; convex then plane; splitting at the edges; covered with tiny, adpressed, brown scales; margins striate, pinkish.

FLESH Pinkish white; thin.

GILLS Pallid, then pink; adnate to decurrent; crowded.

STEM To 10 cm; concolourous with the **cap** below the ring; lighter above; may be a little bulbous at the base; ring thin, brownish.

SPORES 10–12 x 7.5–8 μm; white; smooth; elliptical; basidia 4-spored.

SMELL None. TASTE Not recorded.

HABITAT Caespitose on dead wood or at the base of stumps.

NSW

NOTE See notes as for *A. luteo-bubalina*

Armillaria luteobubalina Watling & Kile.

CAP To 10 cm; colour variable, yellow-brown, reddish, creamy or greenish yellow; convex then plane or even slightly repand; margin usually inrolled.

FLESH White; thin.

GILLS White then pallid-brown; close; adnate to decurrent.

STEM To 20 cm; brownish; thick; tough; fibrillose exterior; solid or pithy; annulus fixed, white, membranous, pendulous.

SPORES 7.5–9 x 5–6.5 μm; white; smooth; elliptical; iodine negative; basidia 4-spored.

SMELL None. TASTE More or less bitter.
HABITAT In dense, caespitose clusters at the bases of trees; parasitic.
QLD NSW VIC SA WA
NOTE Two other species are common:
A. novae-zelandiae (Stevenson) Boese-
winkel has a viscid cap, *A. fumosa* has a
deep grey cap with no yellow squa-
mules and a distinctly two zoned cortina instead of a true membranous ring.

Bolbitius variicolor Atk.

CAP To 3 cm; tawny-yellow to lemon
yellow becoming fawn-grey; globose
then conico-convex finally plane;
translucent; viscid; margin striate or
plicate; cuticle cellular.
FLESH Thin; grey; watery.
GILLS Pallid fawn then brown; free;
close.
STEM To 3 cm; pallid straw-yellow;
very thin; smooth; hollow; no ring or
volva; easily detached from cap.
SPORES 10.5–12.5 x 7.5–9.5 μm;
brown; smooth; with germ pore;
basidia 4-spored.
SMELL None. TASTE None.
HABITAT Gregarious on very rich
soil, especially manured lawns; caps
shrivel up to form a gelatinous blob.
WA

Chlorophyllum molybdites (Meyer : Fr.) Mass.

CAP To 12 cm; brownish white or
cream with concentric rings of dark,
brown scales; globose, then conical
finally umbonate; cuticle peels; margin frequently splitting.

POISONOUS

FLESH White; thick; reddening rapidly on cutting.
GILLS Pallid green then grey-green;
crowded; free.
STEM To 8 cm; greyish to blackish,

white at the base; bulbous; hollow
or pith filled; surface satiny smooth;
no volva

FLESH White, reddening rapidly on
cutting; readily detached from cap;
ring fixed, brownish white, membranous, splitting into an upper and
lower section.

SPORES 11–11.5 x 8–8.5 μm; grey
olive-green; oval; smooth; dextrinoid; basidia 4-spored.

SMELL None. TASTE None. Poisonous.

HABITAT Gregarious on lawns or in
pastures.

QLD NSW WA NT

Clitocybe eucalyptorum Clel.

CAP To 12 cm; greyish brown to
brown, often discoloured; convex,
then plane, finally repand; dry; margin inrolled.

FLESH White; thick.

GILLS Grey to cream; close; more or
less decurrent.

STEM To 8 cm; pallid grey-brown;
stout; hollow; no ring or volva; a
whitish bloom often present.

SPORES 5–6.5 x 4–5 μm; white;
smooth; spherical to pear-shaped.

SMELL None. TASTE Not recorded.

HABITAT On soil, amongst eucalypt
litter.

NSW VIC

Clitocybula aff. *cyathiformis var. cinerascens* Fr.

CAP To 3.5 cm; greyish brown to
pale grey; umbilicate to more or less
infundibuliform; dry; striate; translucent.

FLESH Very thin; grey.

GILLS Grey-white; decurrent; moderately close.

STEM To 8 cm; pale greyish white or
brownish; hollow; slender; tough; no

ring or volva; not readily detached from cap.

SPORES 7–8 x 4–5 μm; white; smooth; more or less pear-shaped.

SMELL None. **TASTE** Not recorded.

HABITAT Caespitose on rotten wood.

NSW

Collybia aff. *butyracea* (Bull.: Fr.) P. Kumm.

CAP To 6 cm; warm biscuit-brown to creamy brown; convex to almost plane but with the margins strongly inrolled; cuticle filamentous; surface smooth and greasy to touch.

FLESH Thin; white.

GILLS Pallid, then concolorous with cap; close; adnate to slightly sinuate.

STEM To 6 cm; pallid brown to dark brown; solid; tough; not readily detached; no ring or volva.

SPORES 7.5–9 x 5–5.5 μm; white; smooth; elliptical; apiculus prominent; basidia 4-spored.

SMELL None. **TASTE** Not recorded.

HABITAT In troops amongst grass and litter at the bases of gum-trees; often on buried wood chips.

VIC SA WA NSW

NOTE This species seems to be closely related to the European species *C. butyracea*. Until further comparisons of the Australian and European plants are made, Cleland's name is retained.

Collybia elegans Clel.[= *Marasmius elegans* (Clel.) Grgurinovic]

CAP To 2.5 cm; deep brown or tan, paler at the margin; hemispherical then convex; smooth; dry; margin faintly striate.

FLESH White to creamy brown; thin.

GILLS Creamy coloured; adnexed; crowded.

STEM To 6 cm; pale superiorly darkening to deep brown below;

hollow; the base is decorated with bristly white fibres; no ring or volva; surface polished; texture flexible and tough.

SPORES 9–11 x 4.5–5.5 µm; white; pointed at one end; smooth; no iodine reaction; basidia 4-spored.

SMELL Recorded as unpleasant but not noted by the author.

TASTE Not recorded.

HABITAT On or amongst leaf litter; gregarious to sub-caespitose.

NSW VIC SA QLD

Collybia fusipes (Bull. : Fr.) Quel.

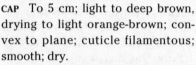

CAP To 5 cm; light to deep brown, drying to light orange-brown; convex to plane; cuticle filamentous; smooth; dry.

FLESH Yellowish; thin.

GILLS Rusty brown, often with brown spots on maturity; adnate; broad; distant.

STEM To 10 cm; pallid superiorly, but soon becoming dark brown towards the base; very finely velvety; deeply grooved longitudinally; hollow; no ring or volva; not de-tachable from cap; rooting base present.

SPORES 4.5–6 x 2.5–4.5 µm; white; smooth; elliptical; no iodine reaction; basidia 4-spored.

SMELL None. TASTE Not recorded.

HABITAT Directly on wood; if it appears on the soil, then buried wood is beneath; often forms large caespitose clusters at tree bases; many stems fuse together to form a large common rooting base.

QLD NSW WA

Collybia velutipes (Curt.: Fr.) P. Kumm.

CAP To 8 cm; yellow-ochre; convex, then plane and finally repand; smooth; viscid; cuticle filamentous.

FLESH White to creamy brown; thin.

GILLS Pale yellow, then brown; adnexed; close to distant.

STEM To 7 cm; pale yellow superiorly then soon brown to dark brown inferiorly; twisted; very tough; densely velvety; no ring or volva; not detachable from cap.

SPORES 6.5–10 x 3–4 μm; white; smooth; no iodine reaction; basidia 4-spored.

SMELL Unpleasant.

TASTE Insipid. Supposedly edible but not recommended.

HABITAT In dense caespitose clusters on dead wood; occasionally on living trees.

QLD NSW VIC SA

Conocybe crispa (Longyear) Sing.

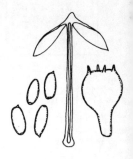

CAP To 3 cm; light buff, darker at the centre; acutely conical; cuticle cellular; dry; smooth; margins striate and cracking.

FLESH Tan; thin.

GILLS Brown; ascending-adnate; no cystidia observed.

STEM To 7.5 cm; 2 to 3 mm thick; white above, brownish below; mealy and a little striate near the gills; bulbous; hollow; not readily detachable from cap; no ring or volva.

SPORES 11–17 x 7.5–9.5 μm; rusty brown; elliptical; smooth; with germpore; basidia 4-spored.

SMELL None. **TASTE** Not recorded.

HABITAT In twos or threes or solitary on lawns, esp. buffalo grass.

NSW VIC SA

Conocybe lactea (Lange) Metrod.
This is almost certainly Cleland's *Galera crispa* Longyear.

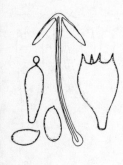

CAP To 2 cm; milky white, may have honey brown tints, conical; cuticle cellular; dry; smooth; margins striate.

FLESH Tan; thin; watery.

GILLS Brown; ascending-adnexed; moderately close; pin-headed marginal cystidia present.

STEM To 10 cm; white, may be brown earth-stains at the base; bulbous; hollow; smooth; no ring or volva; not readily detached.

SPORES 13–19 x 7.5–10.5 μm; brown;oval; smooth; with germpore; basidia 4-spored.

SMELL None. TASTE Not recorded.

HABITAT On lawns, often in large troops.

NSW VIC SA

Coprinus atramentarius (Bull. :Fr.) Fr.

DO NOT
CONSUME
WITH
ALCOHOL

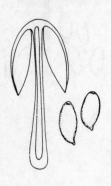

CAP To 8 cm; dirty pale brownish grey, more or less scaly at the centre; campanulate or conical, but becoming upturned as auto-digestion proceeds; cuticle cellular; margin striate; rapidly self-digesting to an inky-black liquid at maturity.

FLESH White; thin; auto-digesting.

GILLS White, becoming black; free; crowded; self-digesting to an inky-black fluid.

STEM To 10 cm; white to brownish below; may be furrowed or fibrillose; base more or less bulbous; often with a ring-like zone; no volva; readily detached.

SPORES 7–10 x 5–6 μm; black; oval; smooth; basidia 4-spored.

SMELL Fungousy. TASTE Pleasant, mild. Edible and good if used before the gills commence to liquefy; **do**

not consume with alcohol as this may cause nausea.

HABITAT Clustered or caespitose; amongst grass or near well rotted tree stumps.

NSW VIC SA

Coprinus comatus (Mull. : Fr.) S.F. Gray

COMMON NAME Lawyers Wig.

CAP To 5 cm diameter and up to 10 cm long; white to cream coloured and covered in shaggy brown scales; resembles an elongated drumstick; cuticle peels; dry or a little sticky in wet weather; margin with ring fragments; auto-digests to an inky-black fluid.

FLESH White; very thin; auto-digesting.

GILLS White becoming pinkish and then black, finally auto-digesting (this process starts from the lower end of the gills and upwards); free; crowded; abundant cylindrical cystidia.

STEM To 15 cm; white; more or less bulbous; hollow with a central thread; usually with a movable ring, but this may disintegrate; no volva; brittle; easily detached from cap.

SPORES 12–14 x 7–9 μm; black; oval; smooth; basidia 4-spored.

SMELL Mild.

TASTE Mild. Edible and very good if used before the gills liquefy. **Do not consume with alcohol** as this may cause nausea.

HABITAT In troops on very rich soil, often where vegetable rubbish has been buried.

QLD NSW VIC TAS SA WA

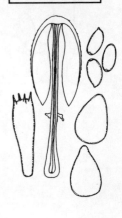

DO NOT CONSUME WITH ALCOHOL

Coprinus disseminatus (Pers. : Fr.) S.F. Gray

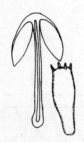

CAP To 2 cm; ochre-brown, fading to ochre-grey except at the centre; campanulate; cuticle cellular; dry; finely mealy; surface plicate.

FLESH Pale tan; very thin.

GILLS Pallid, then purplish grey, finally chocolate-black; crowded; almost no auto-digestion; ascendingly adnate; cystidia present.

STEM To 3 cm; white, but brownish at the base; slender; brittle; hollow; no ring or volva.

SPORES 8–11 x 4–5 μm; black, but violet-brown under the microscope; elliptical; smooth; germ pore present; basidia 4-spored.

SMELL None. TASTE Mild.

HABITAT In dense clusters or troops, often up to a square metre in area; on buried rotting wood, sawdust or against stumps.

QLD NSW VIC TAS SA WA

NOTE Often placed in *Psathyrella* (Fr.) Quel.

Coprinus impatiens (Fr.) Quel.

CAP To 2.5 cm; grey with a brownish umbo; campanulate becoming planar; cuticle cellular; dry; plicate; partly auto-digests to become papery and thin.

FLESH Greyish or brownish; very thin.

GILLS Dull ochre, then black; free, but meeting in a tiny collar at the stipe; partly auto-digesting.

STEM To 6 cm; white; fragile; hollow; no ring or volva; readily detached from cap.

SPORES 17–19.5 x 13–16 μm; black; oval; germ-pore present; basidia 4-spored.

SMELL Mealy. TASTE Mild.

HABITAT In humus or rich soil; in twos or threes but not caespitose.

WA NSW

Coprinus plicatilis (Curt. : Fr.) Fr.

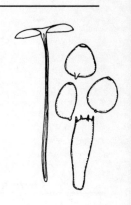

CAP To 2 cm; dull brown becoming grey except at the centre; campanulate becoming plane; dry; cuticle cellular; surface plicate; becoming very thin and papery.

FLESH White to greyish brown; very thin.

GILLS Greyish finally black; edges at first white; moderately distant; attached to a collar at the apex of the stem; scarcely self-digesting.

STEM To 6 cm; white; hollow; brittle; no ring or volva; base slightly bulbous.

SPORES 9.5–13 x 9–11 μm; black; oval to heart-shaped in different perspectives; smooth; basidia 4-spored.

SMELL None. TASTE None.

HABITAT Solitary; on soil amongst grass and plants, in lawns beside paths; rapidly wilting and disappearing in sunlight.

QLD NSW VIC TAS SA WA

Coprinus truncorum (Schaeff.) Fr.

CAP To 3 cm; light tan and densely frosted with white floccules which disappear as the cap matures; campanulate; cuticle cellular; dry; margin usually lobed but becoming ragged and black as auto-digestion proceeds; surface plicate.

FLESH White to tan coloured; thin; auto-digesting.

GILLS Pallid then pinkish and finally black; free; crowded; margins white and finely serrate; large cylindrical cystidia present; auto-digesting.

STEM To 5 cm; white; brittle; hollow; small, velvety hairs at the base; no ring or volva; easily detached from cap.

SPORES 7.5–12 x 6–7 μm; black; elliptical; smooth; with germ pore; basidia 4-spored.

SMELL None. TASTE Mild.

HABITAT In dense clusters, 30 to 40 cm in diameter; caespitose; in grass or leaf mould usually at the foot of dead or dying trees. (Parasitism is suspected of this species by some mycologists.)

QLD NSW VIC TAS SA WA

Cortinarius aff. *albo-violaceus* (Pers. : Fr.) Fr.

To 7 cm; pale grey-lilac; convex finally umbonate; cuticle dry, fibrillose; margin silky-striate.

FLESH White to pallid lilac, especially at stem apex; thick.

GILLS Light lilac to bluish becoming cinnamon; adnexed; more or less distant.

STEM To 8 cm; faintly bluish above the cortina zone but with a whitish bloom below; solid; dry; cortina white.

SPORES 8–10 x 4.5–5 μm; brown; oval; punctate; basidia 4-spored.

SMELL None.

TASTE Pleasant. Supposedly edible; Australian plants have not been tested.

HABITAT In small groups amongst leaf litter.

NSW VIC

Cortinarius archeri Berk.

CAP To 8 cm; deep violet then brownish; convex becoming irregularly folded and somewhat repand; very glutinous and slimy.

FLESH White or violet tinted; thin.

GILLS Brown, violet tinted; adnate to sinuate; a network of veins is present on the gill sides; crowded, cheilocystidia present.

STEM To 8 cm; cortina lilac tinted and very viscid to slimy; stem deep violet blue below the cortina, paler lilac above, very viscid to glutinous, base bulbous; hollow.

SPORES 11.5–13 x 6.5–8 μm; dark brown; oval; punctate; basidia 4-spored.

SMELL None. **TASTE** Not recorded.

HABITAT On soil amongst plant debris. QLD NSW VIC SA WA

NOTE Two other species exist which are similar: ***C. subarcheri*** and ***C. microarcheri.*** Cleland gives the differences as follows:

C. subarcheri spores: 8–10.5 x 4.5–6.5 μm

C. microarcheri spores: 5.5–8.5 x 4.5–5 μm

The overall sizes of the plants are also progressively less. So far the author has only collected *C. archeri*. It is possible the other two species are simply sub-varieties of *C. archeri* but this is not certain.

Cortinarius austrovenetus Clel.

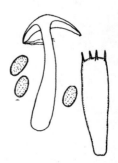

CAP To 7 cm; dark green; convex to planar; cuticle smooth to fibrillose; dry.

FLESH Thin; white.

GILLS Yellow-ochre then brownish; adnate to sinuate; close.

STEM To 7 cm; yellow-ochre tinted; often with a zone of brownish cortina fragments; stout; attenuated upwards; hollow; dry.

SPORES 9.5–13 x 5.5–6.5 μm; brown; oval; punctate; basidia 4-spored.

SMELL None. **TASTE** Not recorded.

HABITAT Single or in troops amongst eucalyptus litter; on soil.

NSW VIC SA

Cortinarius aff. *cinnabarina* Fr.

CAP To 4 cm; deep cinnabar (red-lead') but not blood-red or scarlet; convex; smooth or even shining; dry; cuticle filamentous.

FLESH Red; thin.

GILLS Dark red-lead; adnate; rather distant.

STEM To 5 cm; concolorous with cap; slender; cortina concolorous; dry.

SPORES 7.5–9 x 4.5–5.5 μm; brown; oval; punctate; basidia 4-spored.

SMELL Of radish. TASTE Of radish.

HABITAT Amongst leaf litter in open forest.

NSW VIC SA

Cortinarius aff. *sanguineus* (Wulf : Fr.) Fr.

CAP To 4 cm; dark blood-red; convex becoming plane; dry; cuticle filamentous; smooth; margins sometimes faintly striate.

FLESH Pallid red; thin; exudes a reddish juice if pressed.

STEM To 8 cm; dark blood-red, paler above; hollow; slender to stout; dry; fibrillose surface; cortina red.

SPORES 6–9 x 4–6 μm; brown; oval to pear-shaped; punctate; basidia 4-spored.

SMELL Of radish. TASTE Not recorded.

HABITAT On soil or very well rotted wood, in forests.

NSW SA VIC

Cortinarius aff. *violaceus* (L. : Fr.) Fr.

CAP To 10 cm; deep violet; convex to umbonate; dry; smooth to scaly (minutely so).

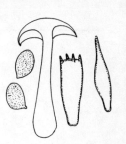

FLESH Blue, becoming white; moderately thick.

GILLS Deep violet, finally dark-brown; very broad; adnate; distant; connected by veins.

STEM To 10 cm; deep violet; stout; bulbous; tomentose then fibrillose; cortina blue finally rusty from the spores.

SPORES 10–11 x 7.5–8 μm; brown; oval; punctate; basidia 4-spored.

SMELL Like cedar. **TASTE** Mild or none.

HABITAT On soil amongst litter in sheltered forest areas.

NSW VIC

NOTE Acutely tipped cystidia on gills are very prominent. This will most likely not be the Friesian species. The author collected this species in the Kur-in-gai Chase area. The cedar smell that is characteristic of the European species is not present in Australian plants. Many of the Cortinarii are mycorrhizal, and it would be unlikely to find the same species attached to the roots of both Australian and European trees.

Crepidotus applanatus (Berk. & Curt.) Sacc.[= *Crepidotus globigerus* Berk. sensu Cleland]

CAP To 7 cm; white to pale cinnamon; dry; bracket to fan-shaped; smooth, fragile.

FLESH White; very thin, watery.

GILLS White then brown; crowded; radial.

STEM Lateral, rudimentary or absent.

SPORES 6–7.5 μm; brown; globose, very finely punctate; basidia 2-spored.

SMELL None. **TASTE** Bitter.

HABITAT On dead rotting logs, sticks, etc.

NSW SA WA

Crepidotus eucalyptorum Clel.

CAP To 4 cm; yellowish brown; fan-shaped; convex; cuticle finely velvety; dry; margins often a little inturned.

FLESH White; attenuated outwards.

GILLS Pallid brown; close; radial.

STEM Lateral, rudimentary or non-existent.

SPORES 7.5–11 x 5.5–7.5 μm; pale brown; oval; smooth; basidia 4-spored.

SMELL None. TASTE Bitter.

HABITAT On the bark of living eucalypts.

NSW VIC SA

Crepidotus prostratus Clel.

CAP To 8 cm; tawny-yellow to brownish, often brown stained from the spores that have fallen from overlapping caps; very irregular and lobed, cracked, but more or less convex; dry; margins inrolled.

FLESH White; thick.

GILLS Orange-yellow then yellow-brown; crowded; rather decurrent.

STEM Excentric or absent, concolorous with cap if present.

SPORES 8–9.5 x 4.5–5.5 μm; brown; oval; smooth; basidia 4-spored.

SMELL Strong, musty. TASTE Not recorded.

HABITAT Caespitose at the base of stumps; overlapping and forming masses of about 20 cm diameter.

NSW VIC SA WA

Cyptotrama asprata (Berk.) Redhead & Ginns.
[= *Armillaria asprata* (Berk.) Petch]

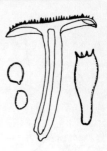

CAP To 6 cm; pale yellow to reddish orange; covered in large, orange-red, conical warts; globose then convex, finally plane; warts disappearing as the cap expands, but clusters remain at the centre.

FLESH White; thin.

GILLS White; adnate; close; cystidia present.

STEM To 6 cm; pale yellow near the gills, punctate orange near the base; stuffed then hollow; veil cobwebby to membranous.

SPORES 7–8 x 5–6 μm; white; smooth; sub-globose.

SMELL None. **TASTE** Not recorded.

HABITAT On rotting wood.

QLD NSW VIC SA

Entoloma moongum Grgurinovic

CAP To 2 cm; very dark brown with tints of steel blue; umbilicate with the margins inrolled where the cap may also be more or less striate; smooth.

FLESH Very thin; concolorous with cap.

GILLS Pure white becoming pink; adnate to very slightly decurrent; the decurrent state being more noticeable when young.

STEM To 2.5 cm; to 3 mm thick; hollow; dark steel blue with white patch at the base; sometimes more or less flattened.

SPORES 10.5–12.5 x 6.5–7.5 μm; angular; apiculus very prominent; spore print pink.

HABITAT Gregarious upon soil amongst grass.

NSW VIC SA

Entoloma virescens (Berk. & Curt.) E. Horak

CAP To 2.5 cm; conical with pronounced umbo; intense, deep sky blue; dry; finely matte surface; margins in-curled, hiding the gills.

FLESH Concolorous with cap; very thin.

GILLS Ascending; moderately crowded; bright lavender blue, tinted reddish.

STEM To 8 cm; somewhat twisted and hence longitudinally striate; dry; deep blue sometimes with faint ochre tints; no ring or volva.

SPORES 10–12 μm; polygonal, usually appearing as intertwined cubes; apiculus 1.5–2.5 μm; pink in mass.

SMELL Faint. TASTE Not recorded.

HABITAT Singly or in twos on soil in forest.

NSW QLD

NOTE Uncommon, but included here as an unmistakable member of a very difficult genus. (Also in New Zealand.)

Gymnopilus pampeanus (Speg.) Singer

CAP To 7.5 cm; warm brown to gold; convex; cuticle filamentous; dry; minutely radially fibrillose; margins inrolled when young; often irregular with maturity.

FLESH Light tan; thick.

GILLS Bright yellow, finally brown; adnate; crowded; cystidia present.

STEM To 7 cm; pallid brown; fibrillosely striate; stout; solid; yellowish or brownish cortina present which may occasionally thicken to give a ring-like appearance.

SPORES 6.5–8 x 4–5.5 μm; brown;

oval; punctate; basidia 4-spored.

SMELL None. TASTE Bitter.

HABITAT Solitary or gregarious, but always on wood which may some-times be buried so the plants appear to be directly on soil.

WA NSW QLD.

Gymnopilus purpurata (Cooke & Mass.) Sing.

CAP To 5 cm; purplish reddish brown becoming brown with pur-plish red tints; convex; dry; cuticle filamentous; a hand lens reveals that the cap surface is covered with minute fibrillose warts.

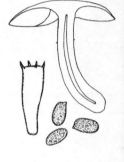

FLESH Yellow; thick.

GILLS Golden finally orange-brown; adnate to sinuate or even a little decurrent; crowded.

STEM To 8 cm; pale straw-yellow above, brown below; more or less smooth; tough; hollow; cortina vari-able and may form a yellowish-brown stained ring with spore deposits.

SPORES 8.5–9.5 x 6–6.5 μm; ochre-brown; oval; punctate; basidia 4-spored.

SMELL None. TASTE Bitter.

HABITAT Gregarious to caespitose on fallen, dead timber.

WA SA

NOTE This is Cleland's *Flammula pur-purata* Cke & Mass.; however, the punctate spores place the species into the genus *Gymnopilus*.

Hebeloma hiemale Bres.

CAP To 5 cm; brownish grey drying to pallid fawn, often appearing as if a whitish film lies over the cap sur-face; convex often repand; viscid; cuticle filamentous.

MILDLY
POISONOUS

FLESH White; thick.

GILLS Pallid then brownish; sinuate to adnate; crowded.

STEM To 4 cm; white; brownish at the base; stout; hollow; more or less smooth; no ring or volva; not readily detached.

SPORES 13–14 x 7–8 μm; brown; oval; punctate; basidia 4-spored.

SMELL None. TASTE Bitter. Mildly poisonous, but probably not dangerous to a healthy person.

HABITAT Amongst fallen needles of introduced species of *Pinus* especially *P. radiata*; on soil; gregarious.

WA SA VIC NSW

Hebeloma mesophaeum (Pers.) Quel.

CAP To 4 cm; date-brown, paler at the margins; convex to a little umbonate; viscid; cuticle filamentous.

FLESH Pale brown; thin.

GILLS Pallid then cigar-brown; sinuate; close.

STEM To 4 cm; pallid or tinted brownish; slender; brittle, hollow; fibrillose; no volva; traces of a veil may remain on the upper stem.

SPORES 9–11 x 4.5–5.5 μm; brown; oval; minutely punctate to almost smooth; basidia 4-spored.

SMELL None. TASTE Bitter.

HABITAT On soil amongst needles; always with introduced species of pines esp. *P. radiata*.

NOTE Cleland describes this species and its variety *minus* Cke. from SA and NSW respectively.

Hygrocybe astatogala (Heim ex Heim) Heinemann

CAP To 3 cm; colour very variable red, orange or yellow (sometimes greenish tinted), often overlain with

sooty black, and eventually more or less black with only a few colour tints: more or less conical and finally broadly conical; dry, smooth, but covered with radial, black fibrils; margins even.

FLESH Reddish orange to yellow; very thin; exudes a clear to yellow tinted, watery fluid when cut and rapidly turns black on exposure to air or with bruising.

GILLS Yellow to orange; waxy; ascending to more or less free, distant, thick, bruise black upon injury.

STEM To 8 cm; very pale yellow to orange, may have red tints; white at the base; dry, cylindrical, hollow, more or less covered with black fibrils; rapidly bruising black on injury.

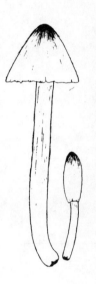

SPORES 7.5–10.0 x 6–8.5 μm; subglobose,; hyaline; thin walled; iodine gative; frequently with dark contents.

SMELL None. **TASTE** Mild.

HABITAT Solitary or in 2s or 3s on soil amongst forest leaf litter; often in very sheltered and moist locations.

QLD NSW VIC TAS

NOTE This species has often been mistaken in the past for *H. conica* which it resembles, except for fibrils and watery fluid that appears from the cut flesh.

Hygrocybe cantharellus (Schwein.) Murrill

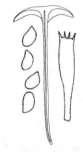

CAP To 3 cm; orange becoming scarlet but fading with age; convex to planar; dry; margins even, scalloped or wavy.

FLESH Reddish orange to yellow; thin.

GILLS Orange to yellow, paler than the cap; waxy; decurrent; distant.

STEM To 9 cm; concolorous or paler than the cap; slender; hollow; no ring or volva; dry.

SPORES 8–10 x 5–6 μm; white; elliptical; smooth; iodine negative; basidia 2
or 4-spored.

SMELL None. TASTE Mild.

HABITAT Gregarious amongst leaf litter, moss or grass.

NSW QLD

Hygrocybe cheelii A.M. Young [= *Cantharellus lilacinas* Clel. & Cheel.]

CAP To 3 cm; pink-lilac; convex,
smooth but finely velvety under a
x10 lens, dry.

FLESH Thick, white with lilac tints.

GILLS Mauve lilac, decurrent; often
branching near the cap margins.

STRIPE To 5 cm; pink mauve to lilac, yellow at the base; dry; solid.

SPORES 6.7–8.7 x 4.7–6.3 μm; white;
ellipsoid; smooth.

HABITAT On soil amongst leaf litter in
forest

SA VIC NSW

Hygrocybe chromolimonea T.W. May & A.E. Wood

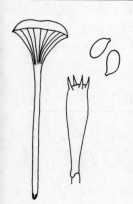

CAP To 2 cm; bright chrome-yellow;
convex but with centre depressed; viscid to glutinous.

FLESH Chrome yellow; watery; thin.

GILLS Chrome yellow; decurrent; with
glutinous thread on margins (use x10
lens).

STEM To 3.5 cm; bright chrome-yellow;
smooth; viscid to glutinous.

SPORES 7.5–10.0 x 4.5–6.0 μm; white;
smooth; ellipsoid; basidia 4-spored.

SMELL None. TASTE None.

HABITAT Gregarious amongst moss or
litter in forests; often on old tree fern
bases.

VIC NSW

Hygrocybe conica (Schaeff. :Fr.) P. Kumm.

CAP To 7 cm; colour extremely variable, pale orange or yellow to bright red — often yellow with red splashes, or red with black patches or black with red patches; occasionally there may even be greenish or olive tints (WA specimens seem to be a yellowish variety with red splashes, while NSW has a reddish or black strain); always acutely conical, especially in the early stages; very slightly viscid when moist; margins lobed, broken or cracking; surface generally blackens with age or very quickly when bruised.

FLESH Concolorous with cap; very thin; waxy; blackens in air when cut.

GILLS White, becoming grey, pale yellow or a pallid cap hue, often with rosy tints; blacken when bruised; margins often ragged; waxy; more or less free or ascending; crowded.

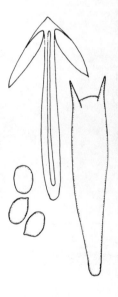

STEM To 11 cm; colour varies from dark red to pale yellow, base often more or less white; blackens when bruised or cut or in old age; moist but not viscid; hollow; fragile; often splitting; twisted and longitudinally striate; no ring or volva; not detachable.

SPORES 11–13 x 5.5–6.5 μm; white; oval; smooth; no iodine reaction; basidia 1, 2, 3 or 4-spored.

SMELL None. **TASTE** Mild. Supposedly edible **but not recommended.**

HABITAT Gregarious in buffalo grass lawns.

NSW VIC

NOTE If the specimen has numbers of blackish fibrils on the cap and stem then it may be *H. astatogala* (Heim) Heinemann.

Hygrocybe graminicolor (E. Horak) T.W. May & A.E. Wood

CAP To 3 cm; light grass green but darker at the centre; old specimens may fade/wash to pallid pink with age or heavy rain; convex becoming plane and depressed at the centre or funnel-shaped; smooth; pellucid striate; viscid to glutinous.

FLESH Thin; green.

GILLS White to tinted green, margins slightly grey-green and with a fine glutinous thread along the edge; broadly adnate to subdecurrent, thick, distant; cheilocystidia present along gill margins.

STEM To 4 cm; green sometimes with slight yellowish tints at the base; cylindrical; smooth; viscid to glutinous.

SPORES (5.0) 5.5–7.5 x 3.5–5 μm; ellipsoid to oblong; hyaline; smooth; iodine negative; basidia (2)4-spored.

SMELL Often unpleasant, of burnt grass. **TASTE** Mild.

HABITAT Solitary to gregarious or caespitose on soil in rainforest.

NSW VIC TAS QLD

NOTE *H. graminicolor* is the most common of the two viscid, green taxa.

Hygrocybe kula Grgurinovic

CAP To 2 cm; brilliant crimson; convex then becoming rather flattened and occasionally depressed at the centre; dry; smooth; margins even and not cracking; may be yellow tinted.

FLESH Thin; concolorous.

GILLS Pure white becoming cream with age; broadly adnate with a slight decurrent tooth to deeply decurrent; thick; widely spaced.

STEM To 2 cm; brilliant crimson but paling with age; more or less cylindrical, occasionally becoming flattened; firm; smooth; dry.

SPORES 6.5–7.5 (9.0) x 3.5–5 μm; white; ellipsoid and occasionally slightly constricted medially.

SMELL None. **TASTE** Mild.

HABITAT On soil in rainforest or at least in very sheltered locations; gregarious to caespitose.

SA NSW QLD

NOTE This species differs from *H. miniata* (Fr.: Fr.) Kumm. by having lamellae that are pure white rather than yellow pink. Cleland misidentified this species as a variant of *H. miniatus.*

Hygrocybe lewellinae (Kalch.) A.M. Young

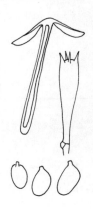

CAP To 3 cm; pale violet, but fading to dull brown and remaining violet only at the margin; conical becoming plane; smooth; not viscid; margin often splitting.

FLESH Concolorous.

GILLS Concolorous with cap; whitish near stem; adnexed becoming more or less free; close; waxy.

STEM To 6 cm; concolorous with cap; more or less slender; smooth; polished; hollow; no ring or volva; not easily detached.

SPORES 7 x 5 μm; white; smooth.

SMELL None. **TASTE** Mild or none.

HABITAT On sandy soil amongst undergrowth.

VIC NSW QLD

Hygrocybe miniata (Fr. : Fr.) P. Kumm.

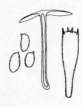

CAP To 3 cm; bright scarlet-red; conical then convex, or slightly umbilicate; moist to very slightly viscid; faintly striate if moist; scurify when dry.

FLESH Orange-red to yellow-orange; waxy; thin.

GILLS Orange-red to yellowish; adnate to adnexed; thick; waxy; distant.

STEM To 5 cm; red, often yellowish at the base; more or less stout; hollow; moist but not viscid; no ring or volva; not detachable from the cap.

SPORES 7–10.5 x 4.5–6.5 μm; white; smooth; elliptical; iodine negative; basidia 2 or 4-spored.

SMELL None. **TASTE** Mild.

HABITAT Gregarious on soil in woodlands or grasslands, usually in sheltered sites.

VIC SA NSW QLD

Hygrocybe rodwayi (Massee) A.M. Young

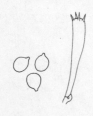

CAP To 2 cm; white but very soon cream coloured with the centre deep cream; convex becoming plane or a little depressed at the centre; smooth; dry; not striate; margins even, not cracking and may be a little inrolled when young.

FLESH Thin; white.

GILLS White; mostly strongly decurrent; thick; widely spaced; veined near the cap; margins even and concolorous.

STEM To 4.5 cm; smooth; dry; white to pallid cream with age; tapering downwards.

SPORES (4.5) 5–7 (7.5) x 4.5–5.5 (6) μm; sub-globose to occasionally globose; white; smooth; iodine negative; basidia 4-spored.

SMELL None. **TASTE** Mild.

HABITAT Gregarious to caespitose on soil often amongst moss in rainforests.

NSW VIC TAS

Hygrocybe subminutula (Murr.) Pegler

CAP To 3 cm; scarlet fading to orange or pale yellow; convex or slightly umbilicate; cuticle translucent and striate if moist; heavily glutinous.

FLESH Scarlet-orange to pale yellow; thin; brittle; waxy.

GILLS Pale pink-orange; waxy; crowded; adnate to slightly decurrent; fragile.

STEM To 6 cm; scarlet but fading; thin; hollow; very glutinous; no ring or volva; not detachable.

SPORES 7.5–10 x 5–6 μm; white; smooth; elliptical; no iodine reaction; basidia 2, 3 or 4-spored.

SMELL None. **TASTE** Mild.

HABITAT Gregarious on soil, rotting logs or humus (the rotting logs must be in the stage where the wood has become a friable soil-like material); usually in sheltered sites.

NSW

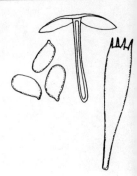

Hygrocybe stevensoniae (Stev.) T.W. May & A.E. Wood

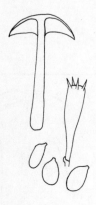

CAP To 3.5 cm; apple green to dark green and always darker at the centre; usually yellowish at the margins; viscid to glutinous; convex expanding to more or less plane in older fruiting bodies, occasionally the centre a little depressed, smooth, pellucid striate in light and dark green for at least half the radius, often completely; margins even or slightly crenulate.

FLESH Thin, dark green.

GILLS Distant, thick, white with greenish tints to more or less pallid green; adnate with decurrent tooth to more or less decurrent; margins concolorous, even and dry.

STEM To 4 cm; green, sometimes yellowish at the base; smooth, viscid to glutinous; cylindrical to flattened; hollow.

SPORES 7–10.5 x 4.5–6 μm; oblong to ellipsoid; smooth; iodine negative; basidia 4-spored.

SMELL None. TASTE Mild.

HABITAT Gregarious on soil in rainforest amongst litter.

NSW QLD

NOTE This species is not as widespread or common as the other closely related green species *Hygrocybe graminicolor*. The two are often confused. Under a microscope, the spore sizes and gill margins readily separate the two; with only a hand lens, the grey, glutinous gill margins of *H. graminicolor* are readily seen.

Hypholoma fasciculare (Huds. : Fr.) P. Kumm.

CAP To 6 cm; greenish, varying from golden brown to orange brown at the

centre to yellow and greenish yellow
at the margin; more or less convex
becoming umbonate and finally
plane; dry; margin at first incurved.

POISONOUS

FLESH Yellow, brownish when cut;
more or less thick.

GILLS Pale sulphur yellow, then
greenish or greenish yellow, finally
olive yellow; adnate to more or less
adnexed; crowded.

STEM To 10 cm; more or less concolorous with the cap, then dirty brown
from the base upwards; smooth but
with a more or less fibrillose zone
from the veil remnants; often contorted; dry; no volva; the veil is very
thin and rapidly disappears.

SPORES 5–7 x 3.5–4.5 μm; purplish
brown; elliptical; smooth; with germ
pore; basidia 4-spored.

SMELL None or fungousy. TASTE Very
bitter. **Poisonous.**

HABITAT Gregarious to caespitose on
decaying logs, stumps etc. If they
appear on the ground, then buried
wood is present.

NSW VIC SA QLD

Hypholoma sublateritium (Fr.) Quel.

CAP To 8 cm; more or less brick-red,
margin paler and may be brownish,
pink or even whitish; more or less
convex becoming plane, but may be
somewhat umbonate; cuticle filamentous; appears moist or watery;
margin at first inrolled with distinct
velar remnants.

FLESH Pallid brown; thick.

GILLS Pallid, then greyish, finally
dark purplish; adnate to adnexed;
close.

STEM To 9 cm; grey then brownish;

fibrillose to more or less scaly below the ring of veil fragments; often staining yellow; solid; no volva.

SPORES 6–7 x 3–4.5 μm; purplish brown to purplish-grey; elliptical; smooth; with germ-pore; basidia 4-spored.

SMELL None. TASTE Mild to a little bitter.

HABITAT On decaying stumps and logs or buried wood; caespitose or gregarious.

SA NSW

Inocybe asterospora Quel.

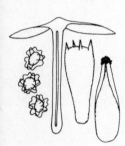

CAP To 4 cm; brown to golden-brown; more or less convex, then umbonate; cuticle rimose; dry.

FLESH Pallid in the cap; brownish in stem.

GILLS Whitish, then cinnamon-brown; adnexed to almost free; more or less close; cystidia present.

STEM To 3 cm; brownish, paler above; slender; bulbous; a little striate; solid; no ring; basal bulb emarginate.

SPORES 9–12 x 7.5–9 μm; brown; nodulose or star-shaped; basidia 4-spored.

SMELL None. TASTE None. **Very poisonous.**

HABITAT Usually solitary on soil in damp, sheltered areas; often beside paths or on banks of earth.

QLD SA WA

Inocybe australiensis Clel. & Cheel.

POISONOUS

CAP To 2 cm; brown; umbonate; rimose; dry; fibrillosely shaggy.

FLESH Brownish; very thin.

STEM To 2 cm; brownish, but covered with white granules; more or less hollow; no ring or volva; base slightly bulbous.

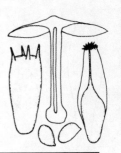

SPORES 8 x 5 μm; brown; elliptical; smooth; basidia 4-spored.

SMELL None. **TASTE** Not recorded. **Poisonous.**

HABITAT Gregarious on soil on banks or beside paths.

SA WA

Inocybe patouillardii Bres.

VERY POISONOUS

CAP To 7 cm; white, then yellowish brown; rapidly pinkish red where cracked or bruised; campanulate expanding to more or less umbonate, then irregularly so, the margin often splitting.

FLESH White, finally pinkish where exposed to the air; thin.

GILLS White, then olive-yellow; adnexed; cystidia present.

STEM To 7 cm; white; tinged with yellowish-brown; smooth; thick; bruises pink; no ring or volva.

SPORES 9.5–12 x 5–8 μm; rusty-brown; smooth; more or less bean-shaped; basidia 4-spored.

SMELL Unpleasant. **TASTE** Not recorded. **Dangerously poisonous.**

HABITAT On soil; gregarious in pine forests, especially introduced species.

NSW ACT

Laccaria lateritia Mal.

CAP To 4 cm; reddish brown to dark reddish brown; corvex to more or less plane on maturity, occasionally a little umbonate; margin more or less striate; moist but not viscid; hygrophanous; very finely scaly when dry.

FLESH Reddish brown; thin.

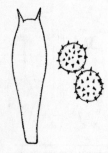

GILLS Flesh-pink with a white, dusty bloom; adnate to adnexed; distant; thick; sometimes faintly violet tinted.

STEM To 5 cm; reddish brown; twisted and a little fibrillose; hollow; no ring or volva.

SPORES 10–12 μm; white; globose; spiny; iodine reaction negative ;basidia 2-spored.

SMELL None. **TASTE** Mild. Edible (supposedly) but **not recommended**. Australian specimens have yet to be tested.

HABITAT Gregarious on soil amongst grass or litter.

WA NSW QLD

NOTE The genus *Laccaria* is extremely difficult in terms of species separation and generally a microscope is essential. Many previous workers have probably lumped all past collections together as *L. laccata*. The author's own studies seem to indicate that *L. laccata* is quite uncommon and the most frequent species is *L. lateritia*, a 2-spored species.

Lacrymaria asperospora (Clel.) Watling [= *Psilocybe asperospora* Clel.]

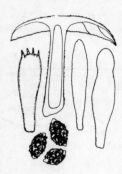

CAP To 5 cm; yellowish brown to date-brown; very fibrillose; convex to more or less umbonate; dry; margin usually with veil fragments.

FLESH Dark brown; thin; watery.

GILLS Dark brown, tinged purplish; often mottled; edges white, serrate; more or less adnate; cystidia present; the gills weep drops of clear liquid in wet weather.

STEM To 5 cm; concolorous with the cap; more or less slender; very fibrillose to shaggy; no ring or volva.

SPORES 8–11 x 5–6 μm; black;

elliptical; very strongly warted; basidia 4-spored.

SMELL None. **TASTE** Mild.

HABITAT Solitary to clustered in rich soil in wether grassland or woodland. NSW SA VIC QLD

Lactarius clarkeae Clel.

CAP To 7 cm; pale orange to salmon-orange or grey-orange; more or less funnel-shaped or sometimes rather convex and umbilicate, but always with the cap margin down turned; surface dry; very finely velvety.

FLESH White; thin; brittle.

LATEX White; milky; mild in taste; readily flows from all parts of the fruiting body when they are bruised or cut.

GILLS Creamy white; adnate to decurrent; more or less distant; occasionally branching near the stem.

STEM To 4 cm; greyish orange to apricot, paler towards the base; solid to slightly hollow; no ring or volva; smooth or minutely velvety.

SPORES 7.5–9 x 6.5–8 μm; white; broadly elliptical; warty, the warts are amyloid; basidia 4-spored.

SMELL None or fishy. **TASTE** Mild.

HABITAT On soil amongst leaf litter; often gregarious; usually found in hilly or mountain areas; in eucalypt forests.

QLD NSW VIC SA WA

Lactarius deliciosus (L. : Fr.) S.F. Gray

CAP To 8 cm; reddish orange, later staining greenish, the colour generally zoned; convex, then depressed, finally funnel-shaped; dry to slightly viscid; margins inrolled. (Occasionally specimens up to 25 cm

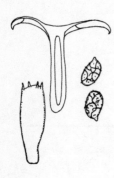

diameter and as much in height.)

FLESH Orange; brittle; thick.

LATEX Orange; mild in taste; exudes from all parts when cut or bruised.

GILLS Reddish orange, later spotted green; decurrent; crowded.

STEM To 6 cm; concolorous with the cap, spotting greenish; stout; no ring or volva.

SPORES 7–9 x 6–7 µm; creamy white; elliptical; surface warty, the warts amyloid and either scattered at random or forming a distinct network; basidia 4-spored.

SMELL None. TASTE Mild to a little bitter. Edible and good, although it requires special cooking to make it palatable.

HABITAT On soil amongst pine needles in plantations of introduced pine species. Mycorrhizal with *Pinus spp.* Usually gregarious.

NSW ACT VIC SA WA

Lactarius aff. *piperatus* (scop. : Fr.) S.F. Gray

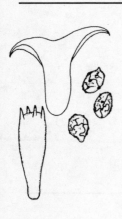

CAP To 12 cm; white; sometimes brown stained; convex, then infundibuliform; smooth; margins inrolled.

FLESH Thick; white; brittle.

LATEX White; milky; copious; exuded from all parts when broken or bruised; *extremely* hot and peppery or acrid.

GILLS White, finally creamy yellow; crowded; decurrent; sometimes branching.

STEM To 5 cm; white; stout; solid; smooth; dry; no ring or volva.

SPORES 6–8.5 x 5.5–6.5 µm; white; sub-spherical with a prominent apiculus; warty, the warts amyloid; basidia 4-spored.

SMELL None. **TASTE** Extremely hot or acrid.

HABITAT In rich soil or humus amongst leaf litter or grass in eucalypt forest or woodland; generally in hilly or mountain regions.

QLD NSW VIC

Lentinellus flabelliformis (Bolt. : Fr.) Ito

CAP To 3 cm; brown to pinkish brown; convex then plane; attached to the substrate laterally at the margin or with an almost non-existent stem; dry; faintly velvety; margin incurved.

FLESH Whitish to brown; thin.

GILLS White to pinkish brown; if a **stem** is present, then they are decurrent, if no stem is present, then the gills radiate from the point of attachment; edges deeply serrate; close.

STEM Degenerate or absent.

SPORES 5–5.5 x 4–5 μm; white; globose or sub-globose; minutely spiny and the spines amyloid, together with the spore wall; basidia 4-spored.

SMELL None. **TASTE** Mild to slightly acrid.

HABITAT Amongst moss on rotting bark of living trees, usually hardwoods; gregarious.

WA NSW QLD

Lentinus fasciatus Berk.

CAP To 5 cm; brown; densely hispid, the short hairs often in clusters; convex then deeply funnel shaped, margins inrolled.

FLESH Very thin; leathery.

GILLS Brownish but usually with a violet hue; decurrent.

STEM To 3 cm; brown; densely hairy; similar to cap.

SPORES 6–9 x 4–5 μm; ellipsoid;
white; smooth; basidia 4-spored.
SMELL None. TASTE Not recorded.
HABITAT On logs or small branches;
often clustered.
QLD NSW SA TAS

Lepiota fimetaria (Cooke & Massee) Sacc. [= *Leuco-agaricus fimetaria* (Locq.) Sing.]

CAP To 9 cm; creamy white with
ochre umbo, some scattered ochre
scales near the centre; umbonate;
margins striate, often with veil remnants.
FLESH Thin; white; may become pinkish in cap tissues, but bright red in
the stem.
GILLS White; free; crowded.
STEM To 10 cm; white; smooth; hollow; thicker at the base but not bulbous; ring is white, fixed, prominent,
and appears double at its edges;
stem base rapidly turns bright red if
cut.
SPORES 8–12 x 6–8 μm; white;
smooth; ellipsoid; dextrinoid; basidia 2-spored.
SMELL Mushroomy. TASTE Mild.
Edibility suspect; **best avoided.**
HABITAT Gregarious amongst grass
or litter; in open areas or woodland.
QLD NSW

Lepiota fuliginosa Clel.

CAP To 7 cm; white with grey-black
scales zoned in rings over the surface and massed at the centre; convex then plane; traces of a veil at the
margin.
FLESH White; thin.
GILLS Creamy white, slightly pink
with age; free; close.
STEM To 6 cm; white; slender; a little

bulbous; ring white, soon evanescent; no volva.

SPORES 6.5–8.5 x 5–6 μm; white; smooth; elliptical; dextrinoid; apiculus very prominent; basidia 4-spored.

SMELL None. **TASTE** None.

HABITAT Gregarious on soil amongst forest litter.

SA WA QLD

Lepiota haemmorhagica Clel.

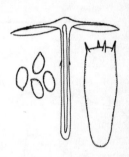

CAP To 5 cm; convex to umbonate, or more or less plane; pallid; covered with minute reddish brown fibrils, and/or fibrillose scales; dry.

FLESH White; slightly reddish in the stem; thin.

GILLS White; stain blood-red on bruising; free; close; the red stains disappear in about twenty minutes.

STEM To 3 cm; white with reddish brown fibrils, slender; hollow; ring small, pallid membranous; no volva; readily detached.

SPORES 5.5–7 x 3.5–5 μm; white; smooth; elliptical; dextrinoid; apiculus very prominent; basidia 4-spored.

SMELL None. **TASTE** Not recorded.

HABITAT On soil amongst leaf litter or grass in open woodland.

WA SA VIC

Lepiota leucothites (Vitt.) T.D. Orton

CAP To 8 cm; white, with brownish or pinkish tinges; spherical then convex becoming umbonate or plane; dry; slightly scaly.

FLESH Thick; white.

GILLS White; but becoming distinctly pinkish with age; free; close.

STEM To 8 cm; white, except for

brownish discolourations at the base; slender; hollow; easily detached; ring fixed, white; no volva.

SPORES 7–9.5 x 5–6 μm; white; smooth; elliptical; dextrinoid; basidia 4-spored.

SMELL Pleasant. **TASTE** Pleasant. Edible and good.

HABITAT Amongst grass; usually gregarious.

WA NSW VIC SA

Macrolepiota dolichaula (Berk. & Br.) Pegler & Rayner.

CAP To 20 cm; whitish to grey-ochre and covered with concentric rings of pale brown or nearly concolorous scales, often the umbo is a little darker; convex then umbonate; at first very like a drumstick; dry; margin often with veil fragments.

FLESH White, thick, unchanging.

GILLS White; crowded; free to remote.

STEM To 20 cm; white, but may be tinged brownish; slender to stout; bulbous; hollow; smooth; easily detached from cap; ring large, white, double, eventually moveable; no volva.

SPORES 12–14.5 x 8–10 μm; white; smooth; elliptical; dextrinoid; basidia 4-spored.

SMELL None to fungousy. **TASTE** Mild.

HABITAT Gregarious on lawns or pastures.

QLD NSW VIC

NOTE There is a lot of confusion around the species group of *M. mastoidea* (Fr.) Kumm., *M. dolichaula* (Berk. & Br.) Sacc., and *M. procera* (Scop. ex Fr.) S.F. Gray. *M. procera* is similar to *M. mastoidea* but the scales are a darker brown and the stem cuticle is brown and cracking into irregular snakeskin-like markings; *M. dolichaula* is also similar to *M. mastoidea* but the scales on the cap remain concolorous with the whitish background, or at most become a very pale brown. A fourth species, *M. rhacodes* (Vitt.) Quel. is almost identical to *M. mastoidea* except that the scales are much darker and coarser and the flesh turns reddish-brown on exposure to air.

Macrolepiota mastoidea (Fr.) P. Kumm.

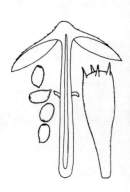

CAP To 6 cm; white with concentric rings of brown scales and the centre totally brown; globular, then conical and finally umbonate; dry.
FLESH White; but turning pinkish especially in the stem.
GILLS White, free; crowded.
STEM To 10 cm; white then brownish; slender; bulbous; hollow; polished and very finely fibrillose; ring white and moveable; no volva; stem easily detached.
SPORES 15–17 x 9–11 μm; white; elliptical; dextrinoid; basidia 4-spored.
SMELL None. **TASTE** Mild, pleasant. Edible.
HABITAT Amongst long grass in woodlands; solitary or gregarious.
WA VIC QLD

Marasmius crinisequi Mueller ex Kalchbr.

CAP To 4 mm; brownish; convex, dimpled at the centre and coarsely striate; usually there is a small bump at the umbilicate centre; dry.
FLESH Brownish; very thin.
GILLS Pallid; adnate; attached to a collar; very few in number.
STEM To 10 cm; blackish brown; smooth; tough; not readily detached;

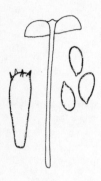

almost hair-like; no ring or volva.

SPORES 7.5–9 x 4.5–5.5 μm; white; smooth; elliptical.

SMELL Not recorded. **TASTE** Not recorded.

HABITAT In plant debris in wet forest gullies; often as a tangled mat of tough, brown mycelial threads growing through the leaf litter.

NSW VIC SA QLD

Marasmius aff. *cinnamoneus* Clel.

CAP To 1 cm; fawn to cinnamon brown; convex to more or less plane; striate when moist but plicate; dry; appears very finely velvety; margins smooth to scalloped.

FLESH Concolorous with cap; thin.

GILLS Light brown; adnate to slightly decurrent; distant.

STEM To 0.8 cm; dark brown to blackish; smooth; tapering downwards; sometimes flattened; no ring or volva.

SPORES 5–6 x 3–4 μm; white; smooth; elliptical to pip-shaped.

SMELL Mild. May smell of garlic when cut. **TASTE** Faintly peppery.

HABITAT Gregarious on bark or rotting branches.

SA NSW

Marasmius oreades (Bolt. : Fr.) Fr.

CAP To 4 cm; pinkish tan to biscuit brown; irregularly convex, becoming plane, but still with a central boss; smooth; dry; margin striate.

FLESH Whitish; thin.

GILLS Pallid cap colour; adnexed to free; sub-distant.

STEM To 7 cm; pale biscuit brown; smooth; whitish and velvety towards the base; rather toughly flexible; no ring or volva.

PLATE 1

Agaricus arvensis

Agaricus campestris

Amanita muscaria

Amauroderma rude

Amanita farinacea

PLATE 2

Amanita preissii

Amanita punctata

Aseroe rubra

Bolbitius variicolor

PLATE 3

Boletellus emodensis

Auricularia aff. auricula-judae

Boletus luteus

Boletus granulatus

Calvatia candida

PLATE 4

Calocera sinensis

Cheilymenia coprinaria

Cantharellus concinnus

Clathrus cibarius

Clathrus pusillus

Clathrus gracilis

PLATE 5

Chlorophyllum molybdites

Coprinus truncorum

Clavulinopsis miniata

Coprinus comatus

PLATE 6

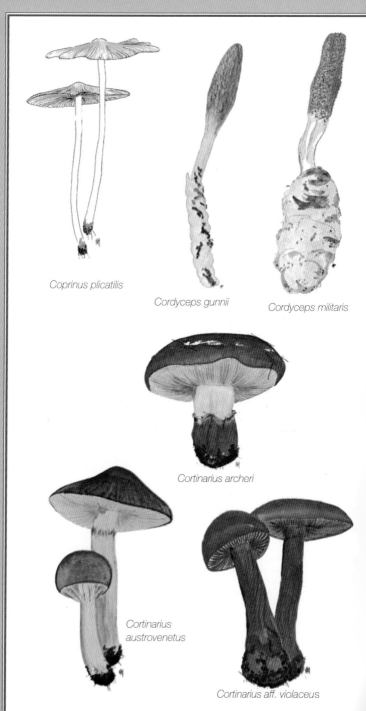

Coprinus plicatilis

Cordyceps gunnii

Cordyceps militaris

Cortinarius archeri

Cortinarius austrovenetus

Cortinarius aff. violaceus

PLATE 7

Cyathus stercoreus

Dictyophora indusiata

Favolus arcularius

Geastrum fenestriatum

Geastrum limbatum

PLATE 8

Hydnum crocidens

Hygrocybe lewellinae

Hygrocybe stevensoniae

Hygrocybe miniatus

Hygrocybe conica

PLATE 9

Conocybe lactea is found on lawns, often in large troops.

PLATE 10

▲ *Banksiamyces toomansis* Beaton & Weste. The genus
Banksiamyces is restricted to dead or very mature *Banksia* cones.
This collection was made on cones of *Banksia serrata* in the Blue
Mountains of New South Wales.
▼ Fairy rings of a species of *Collybia* showing increased growth
of grass in the centre of the ring due to the fungal waste products
acting as a fertiliser.

PLATE 11

▲ *Dictyophora multicolor* is often found in rainforests where it will appear year after year.
▼ *Podaxis carcinomalis* is sometimes found on living termite mounds; it may be symbiotic.

PLATE 12

Coprinus disseminatus is found in dense clusters on buried rotting wood, sawdust, against stumps or on old logs.

PLATE 13

Ramariopsis aff. *ovispora* is a pretty fungus, found on soil or litter in forests.

PLATE 14

▲ *Amauroderma rude* is found on very rotten logs, stumps or buried wood.
▼ *Xeromphalina tenuipes* is found in troops on dead wood or bark.

PLATE 15

▲ *Ganoderma applanatum* (Pers. ex Wallroth) Pat. Many rainforest trees are attacked each year by this parasite which first kills the tree and then uses the dead log as extra food. It has coloured spores which are so prolifically produced that they can dust the surroundings brown.
▼ *Galerina patagonica* is found on rainforest logs.

PLATE 16

Clavaria vermicularis (Fr.) is one of the many clavarioid fungi that
rot leaf litter in forests.

PLATE 17

Hygrocybe cantharellus

Hypholoma fasciculare

Lycoperdon pyriforme

Inocybe asterospora

Laccaria lateritia

PLATE 18

Lacrymaria asperospora

Lactarius clarkeae

Lactarius deliciosus

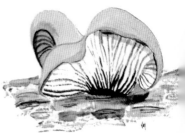

Lentinellus flabelliformis

Macrolepiota konradii

Lepiota fuliginosa

PLATE 19

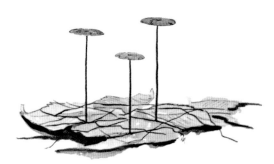

Marasmius crinisequi

Mycena epipterygia

Mycena subgalericulata

Mycena vinacea

Mycena viscidocruenta

PLATE 20

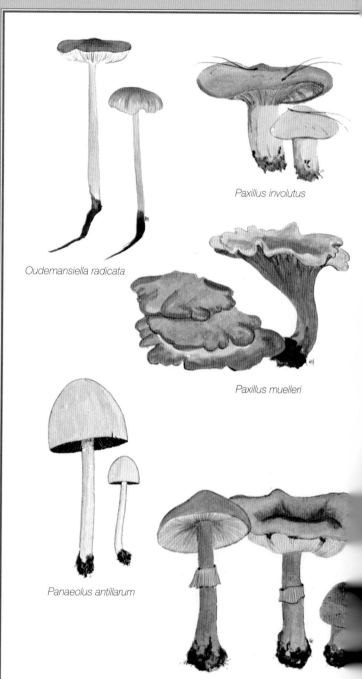

Oudemansiella radicata

Paxillus involutus

Paxillus muelleri

Panaeolus antillarum

Pholiota recedens

PLATE 21

Omphalotus nidiformis

Podaxis pistillaris

Polyporus oblectans

Pluteus atromarginatus

PLATE 22

Psathyrella candolleanum

Psilocybe subaeruginosa

Ramaria fumigata

Entoloma virescens

Russula aff. foetens

Russula mariae

PLATE 23

Russula purpureoflava

Schizophyllum commune

Scleroderma verrucosum

Stropharia rugosoannulata

Trametes cinnabarina

PLATE 24

Tricholoma sublilacinum

Tremellodon gelatinosum

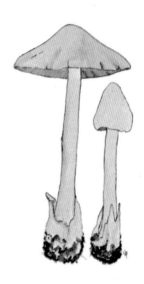

Tulostoma albicans

Volvaria speciosa

PLATE 25

Cyptotrama asprata is found on rotting wood in rainforests.

PLATE 26

▲ *Omphalotus nidiformis* is one of the two common luminescent fungi. Look for it on old eucalypt stumps
▼ *Auricularia delicata* (Fr.) Henn is closely related to other species of *Auricularia*. This species has a vein network under the cap and is found on rainforest logs.

PLATE 27

Cytarria gunnii Berk. is a parasite of several species of *Nothofagus* (Antarctic beech) and is found from Queensland to Tasmania. The fungus erupts from galls on tree branches in spring.

PLATE 28

Hygrocybe cerasinomutata is a gregarious fungus, often found amongst leaf litter, moss or grass.

PLATE 29

Poronia oedipus Mont. is a black species with a swollen stem base found on old cow dung in Queensland and probably New South Wales also.

PLATE 30

▲ *Hypholoma sublateritium* is found on decaying stumps and logs.
▼ *Ramaria subaurantiaca* is found on soil in dense clumps among woodland litter.

PLATE 31

Boletellus emodensis is found on rotting logs and stumps in rainforests.

PLATE 32

Chlorophyllum molybdites is poisonous and found in lawns and pastures. The mature gills become olive green.

SPORES 9.5–10.5 x 5.5–6 μm; white; smooth; more or less elliptical; basidia 4-spored.

SMELL Pleasant. Edible; use caps only— stems are tough. TASTE Sweetish.

HABITAT In lawns or pastures; forms fairy-rings of dead grass.

NSW VIC SA

Mycena aff. *epipterygia* (Scop. : Fr.) S.F. Gray

CAP To 2 cm; greenish to brownish yellow, finally greyish or whitish; occasionally reddish; convex becoming campanulate but always umbonate; viscid; smooth; margins often uneven or torn; striate.

FLESH Yellowish; thin.

GILLS Whitish to slightly yellow; in two tiers; sub-distant; ascending-adnate.

STEM To 6 cm; chrome yellow, fading where exposed; slender; pliant; slimy-viscid, sometimes with large droplets of gluten on the stem; no ring or volva.

SPORES 8–10 x 5–6 μm; white; smooth; elliptical; amyloid; basidia 4-spored.

SMELL None or like cucumber. TASTE Mild.

HABITAT Gregarious upon plant debris.

VIC SA

Mycena pura (Pers. : Fr.) P. Kumm.

CAP To 8 cm; delicate violet to lilac or purple-brown, the violet fading with age; hygrophanous; conical, then broadly umbonate; moist and shiny; margin striate.

FLESH Grey; thin.

GILLS Grey-violet then dusty white; adnate; connected by veins on the cap under-surface; cystidia present.

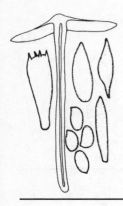

STEM To 10 cm; greyish violet; fibrous; slender; hollow; not readily detached; no ring or volva.

SPORES 6.5–7.5 x 4.5–5 μm; white; smooth; elliptical; amyloid; basidia 4-spored.

SMELL None. **TASTE** Not recorded.

HABITAT In troops amongst pine forest litter; solitary, or caespitose.

WA NSW QLD

Mycena aff. *rorida* (Scop. : Fr.) Quel.

CAP To 1 cm; pallid brown to whitish; convex or with centre depressed; dry; margin strongly striate.

FLESH Whitish; very thin.

GILLS White; adnate to sub-decurrent; distant; very few in number.

STEM To 5 cm; about 1 mm thick; bluish at the top, but soon whitish towards the base, which is more or less brownish; no ring or volva; coated with a thick layer of gluten which persists only at the base as the plant matures; a little strigose at the very base of the stem.

SPORES 8–12 x 4–6 μm; white; smooth; elliptical; amyloid; basidia 2 or 4-spored.

HABITAT Gregarious on casuarina or pine needles; usually in very moist or sheltered positions.

NSW VIC

Mycena sanguinolenta (Alb. & Schw. : Fr.) P. Kumm.

CAP To 1.5 cm; pallid with tinges of reddish brown, darker at the centre; convex to conical becoming broader; at first dusty white from a mealy layer, then smooth and white, but always with the reddish brown tints; margin striate.

FLESH Pallid reddish; thin.

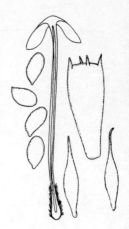

GILLS Pinkish white; margins reddish and serrate; sinuato-adnate; cystidia present.

STEM To 8 cm; white to more or less cap coloured; smooth; hollow; no ring or volva; exudes a prune-coloured or reddish juice when cut; base usually swollen and hispid.

SPORES 8–10 x 4–6 μm; white; sub-elliptical; smooth; weakly amyloid; basidia 4-spored.

SMELL Fungousy. **TASTE** None.

HABITAT Gregarious upon leaf-mould, mossy soil etc. in sheltered areas.

WA VIC SA QLD

Mycena subgalericulata Clel.

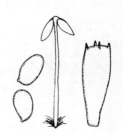

CAP To 3 cm; olive brown to buff brown to greyish; convex to umbonate; dry; smooth; margin striate.

FLESH Concolorous with cap; thin.

GILLS Whitish to greyish; adnate; connected with veins on the undersurface; more or less distant.

STEM To 5 cm; whitish to pallid brown; base hairy white; smooth; more or less polished; no ring or volva.

SPORES 9–13 x 6–8.5 μm; white; smooth; elliptical; basidia 4-spored.

SMELL None. **TASTE** None.

HABITAT In more or less caespitose clusters or gregarious upon trunks, stumps, old logs, etc.

NSW VIC SA QLD

Mycena vinacea Clel.

CAP To 3 cm; pale pink to lilac; conical, then campanulate; dry; smooth; striate.
FLESH White with lilac tints; thin.
GILLS Concolorous with the cap; adnate; close.
STEM To 6 cm; concolorous with the cap; slender; smooth; hollow; hairy at the base; no ring or volva.
SPORES 7.5–13 x 4–8.5 μm; white; smooth; elliptical.
SMELL Strongly of radish. **TASTE** Strongly of radish.
HABITAT In caespitose clusters against stumps on wood etc.
NSW VIC SA QLD

Mycena viscidocruenta Clel. & Cheel

CAP To 1 cm; blood-red; hemispherical, finally a little depressed; striate; viscid; smooth.
FLESH Concolorous with the cap; thin.
GILLS Salmon-pink to a paler blood-red than the cap; adnate to subdecurrent; close; edges slightly darker.
STEM To 2 cm; concolorous with the cap; slender; hollow; viscid to slimy; no ring or volva; usually with a rather fluffy base.
SPORES 7–8.5 x 2.5–3.5 μm; white; smooth; elongated elliptical and with one end pointed.
SMELL Not recorded. **TASTE** Not recorded.
HABITAT On small sticks or leaves in moist bushland esp. gullies.
NSW VIC SA QLD

Naucoria semiorbicularis (Bull. ex St. Amans) Quel.
[= *Agrocybe semiorbicularis* (Bull. ex St. Amans) Fayod]

CAP To 3 cm; brown, drying pallid brown; at first more or less perfectly hemispherical, then convex; smooth; slightly sticky when moist.

FLESH Pallid tan; thin.

GILLS Pallid, then tan or brown; adnate; edges remaining pallid, and also finely serrate; arranged in a three tiered system with shorter intermediate gills between the long main gills (see diagram); cystidia present.

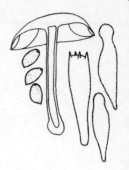

STEM To 6 cm; brownish; slender; hollow; no ring or volva; not readily detached.

SPORES 13–16 x 9–10 μm; cigar-brown; finely punctate; elliptical; basidia 4-spored.

SMELL Like fresh flour. **TASTE** Mild, floury.

HABITAT Gregarious; in troops on soil amongst grass, especially lawns.

NSW VIC SA WA

Omphalina chromacea Clel.

CAP To 1.5 cm; chrome yellow; infundibuliform; translucent and striate, drying pale yellow and opaque; moist-looking but not viscid; smooth.

FLESH Whitish or with tints of the cap; very thin.

GILLS Chrome yellow; decurrent; broad; moderately distant.

STEM To 2 cm; chrome yellow; very slender; rather tough; smooth; solid; no ring or volva; not detachable.

SPORES 7–8 x 3.5–4.5 μm; white; smooth; elliptical; apiculus prominent; iodine negative; basidia 4-spored, occasionally 3-spored.

SMELL None. **TASTE** None.

HABITAT On soil, usually amongst moss, but always in shaded, moist areas.

NSW VIC SA WA

Omphalina fibula (Bull. : Fr.) P. Kumm.

CAP To 1.5 cm; yellowish orange to orange-brown; convex then umbilicate; smooth; slightly striate.

FLESH Concolorous with the cap; very thin.

GILLS Pallid; deeply decurrent; thick; distant.

STEM To 4 cm; concolorous with the cap; very slender; smooth; solid; tough; no ring or volva.

SPORES 4.8–6.5 x 2–2.5 μm; white; smooth; elliptical; iodine negative; basidia 4-spored.

SMELL None. TASTE None.

HABITAT On soil amongst moss, especially in shady moist places.

NSW VIC SA

NOTE What may be *O. pyxidata*, or at least a close species, has been recorded from WA in the Mundaring Dam area. The plants have the typically reddish brown cap with pallid yellow gills, however further collections are needed to confirm this.

Oudemansiella radicata (Relhan : Fr.) Sing. [= *Xerula radicata* (Relhan: Fr.) Dörfelt]

CAP To 6 cm; pale olive to dark brown (a WA variety is at first steel-blue-black, but it expands to the usual pallid brown or dark brown); hemispherical, becoming convex and finally more or less plane; viscid to very slimy; margin more or less striate.

FLESH White; thin.

GILLS White, finally may be pinkish with age; adnate; more or less distant; cystidia present.

STEM To 15 cm; white, brownish at the base; slender; tough; rather twisted; hollow; no ring or volva; striated just below the gills; passing into a long rooting base.

SPORES 15–16 x 10.5–11.5 μm; white; smooth; elliptical; no iodine reaction; basidia 4-spored.

SMELL None. **TASTE** Slightly bitter.

HABITAT On soil over buried wood or at the bases of stumps; generally solitary, but occasionally it has been found in troops where large quantities of wood have been buried.

WA SA VIC NSW QLD

Panaeolus antillarum (Fr.) Dennis [= *P. ovatus* (Cke. & Mass.) Sacc.]

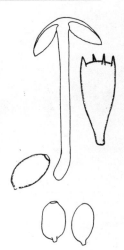

CAP To 8 cm; white with brown tints on aging; parabolic; sticky when moist, more or less viscid when young; smooth; margin exceeding the gills; cuticle often cracking when old.

FLESH White; thin.

GILLS Deep grey, mottled, then black; edges white, serrate; adnate; close.

STEM To 10 cm; white, often stained brown at the base; slender, base a little bulbous; solid; striate near the gills; no ring.

SPORES 13–19 x 8–12 μm; black; oval, to hexagonal; germ pore present; smooth; basidia 4-spored.

SMELL None.

HABITAT On cow or horse manure, or heavily manured soil.

WA VIC NSW QLD

Panaeolus cyanescens (Berk. & Br.) Sacc.

CAP To 4 cm; whitish to pale brown but usually darker at the centre; campanulate or paraboloid; may bruise bluish; smooth.

FLESH Thin; whitish; rapidly becoming

POISONOUS
AND
HALLUCINOGENIC

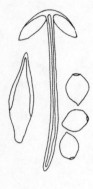

blue on cutting and exposure to air.

GILLS Greyish, finally black; adnate; crowded; with abundant cystidia; the cheilocystidia are more or less cylindrical, hyaline and thin walled; the pleurocystidia are thick walled, brownish, pointed and may have an incrustation at the top.

STEM To 12 cm; up to 4 mm thick; straight; cylindrical; more or less hollow; whitish or brownish at the base; stains blue on bruising; may be longitudinally striate.

SPORES 13–16 x 7–12 μm; black; with germ pore; lens shaped to slightly hexagonal; smooth; basidia 4-spored.

Poisonous and hallucinogenic.

HABITAT On dung.

NT QLD NSW

NOTE The cyanescent tissues and the thick walled cystidia are so unusual that this species is sometimes not placed in the genus *Panaeolus* (Fr.) Quel. and is often called *Copelandia cyanescens* (Berk. & Br.) Sing.

Panaeolus foenisecii (Pers. ex. Fr.) Schroet.

CAP To 3 cm; smooth or a little striate; more or less campanulate; light brown to dark brown.

FLESH Thin; brownish.

GILLS Adnate; close; sooty brown to very dark chocolate; with white edges; cheilocystidia hyaline, crowded.

STEM To 5 cm; slender; whitish to pinkish brown; cylindrical; no ring present; hollow.

SPORES 10–15 x 6–9 μm; elliptical; germ pore present; rough to warted; spore print dark brown, purplish tints may be present; basidia 4-spored.

SMELL Strong to moderate.

HABITAT Gregarious amongst grass, lawns.

WA SA VIC NSW QLD

NOTE This species is often placed in a separate genus, *Panaeolina* Maire, because of its rough spores. Recent work has shown that there exists a series of species with intermediate levels of roughness between *P. foenisecii* and smooth spores. Erection of a separate genus for this species therefore seems unnecessary. There are also conflicting reports about this species' toxicity. Hallucinogenic properties have been noted from SA records and this species should be avoided.

Panaeolus sphinctrinus (Fr.) Quel. (= *P. campanulatus* sensu Cleland, Willis)

CAP To 3 cm; parabolic to campanulate; dark grey drying lighter; brownish, wrinkled forms exist; margin fringed with tooth-like white fragments of the veil.

FLESH Thin; greyish brown.

GILLS Sinuate-adnate; grey then black; crowded; edged with cheilocystidia.

STEM To 12 cm; 2 to 3 mm thick; greyish brown to almost black, maybe paler above; smooth but sometimes pruinose near the gills.

SPORES 12–15 x 7–9 μm; black; with germ pore; smooth; elliptical or somewhat hexagonal; basidia 4-spored.

HABITAT Gregarious on dung, esp. horse.

NSW QLD VIC SA

Paxillus involutus (Batsch : Fr.) Fr.

CAP To 15 cm; more or less olive-brown; convex, then irregularly plane or funnel-shaped; viscid when

VERY POISONOUS

moist; margin strongly inrolled.

FLESH Yellowish brown; thick; soft.

GILLS Yellowish becoming olive-yellow to brown; decurrent; form irregular pores near the stem; readily rubbed off.

STEM To 5 cm; concolorous with the cap; stout; solid; no ring or volva.

SPORES 7.5–11 x 4–6 μm; brown; smooth.

SMELL None. **TASTE** Very poisonous; the poison is cumulative and at first eating seems to have little if any effect.

HABITAT Under introduced species of pine, or English oak.

NSW VIC SA

Paxillus muelleri (Berk.) Sacc.

CAP To 10 cm; bright cadmium yellow to dusty brown, the yellow tints occurring in young or sheltered caps; irregularly funnel-shaped or flabelliform; surface very finely velvety; margins lobed and inrolled.

FLESH Pale yellow, becoming reddish brown when cut; moderately thick.

GILLS Concolorous with cap; deeply decurrent; thick; distant at the stipe but crowded at the margin; often joining to form elongated pores.

STEM To 6 cm; pallid yellow; slender; solid; attenuated basally; no ring or volva.

SPORES 13.5–14.5 x 6–8 μm; brownish in mass, honey-yellow under the microscope; more or less 'mummy-shaped', or like a cigar; smooth; elliptical; basidia 4-spored.

SMELL None. **TASTE** Not recorded.

HABITAT Often caespitose or in clumps amongst leaf litter in eucalyptus woodland.

WA VIC SA

Pholiota recedens (Cooke & Massee) Clel. [= *Descolea recedens* (Cooke & Massee) Singer]

CAP To 4 cm; very dark brown, paling to light brown on drying; hygrophanous; covered in small, light tan floccules when young, but these disappearing on maturity; edge striate if moist.

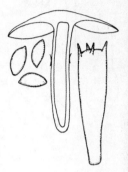

FLESH Pale tan; very thin.

GILLS Pale tan to cinnamon; adnate to adnexed; close.

STEM To 6 cm; brown to dark brown towards the base; slender; hollow; slightly fibrillose; ring fixed, pale tan, very heavily striate or grooved on the upper surface, somewhat pendulous; no volva.

SPORES 11–13 x 7–9 μm; ochre-brown; lemon-shaped and pointed at both ends; very finely punctate; basidia 4-spored.

HABITAT In troops on soil amongst leaf litter.

NSW VIC SA

NOTE The punctate spores of this species immediately remove it from the genus *Pholiota* which has smooth spores; the species is very common however and its inclusion in the key on macroscopic characters yields the result of *Pholiota*. The genus *Descolea* Sing. has been raised to accommodate the peculiar characters of this species. A closely related species *D. maculata* Bougher & Malajczuk is found in Western Australia.

Pholiota aff. *squarrosipes* Clel.

CAP To 6 cm; date-brown or with reddish brown tints, drying pallid tan; at first viscid, drying shiny and fibrillose, the fibrils closely adpressed; convex or a little umbonate;

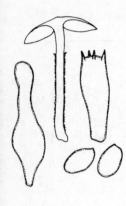

margin occasionally repand.

GILLS Adnate; cinnamon; crowded; cystidia present.

STEM To 12 cm; pale brown at the top, darker below; rough and scaly below the ring, smooth above; ring membranous, very pronounced and pallid brown; no volva.

SPORES 6–8 x 4–5 μm; brown; smooth; elliptical; basidia 4-spored.

SMELL None. **TASTE** Not recorded.

HABITAT Caespitose on or near wood, sometimes forming large clumps.

SA NSW

Pleurotus nidiformis (Berk.) Sacc. [= *P. lampas* (Berk.) Sacc. = *Omphalotus nidiformis* (Berk.) O.K. Miller]

POISONOUS

CAP To 30 cm; golden-brown to creamy or pure white, but usually overlain with streaks or blotches of greyish purple or violet-grey, the colours being rather variable; more or less bracket-shaped to strongly funnel-shaped; moist or dry; margin inrolled.

FLESH White; thick; toughish.

GILLS White; decurrent; crowded; emitting a whitish to yellowish light which weakens in intensity as the plant ages.

STEM To 20 cm; white to purplish, usually concolorous with the cap; attenuated downwards; excentric to lateral; thick; solid; dry; no ring or volva.

SPORES 8.5–9 x 4.5–5 μm; white; smooth; elliptical to oval; iodine negative; basidia 4-spored.

SMELL None. **TASTE** Not recorded.

Poisonous.

HABITAT On old eucalypt stumps or dead trunks; often in huge clusters,

or in tiers up branches; luminous.
WA SA VIC NSW QLD

Pleurotus ostreatus (Jacquin : Fr.) P. Kumm.

CAP To 15 cm; deep greyish blue to almost black, finally brownish; convex to shell-shaped; dry; margin inrolled when young.
FLESH White; thick.
GILLS Whitish; decurrent; crowded.
STEM To 5 cm; white; sometimes hairy at the base; lateral; thick; stout; solid; no ring or volva.
SPORES 10–11 x 3.5–4 μm; white; smooth; elliptical; iodine negative; basidia 4-spored. (British plants are recorded as having a slight lilac tint in the spore print but so far this has not been noted by Australian workers.)
SMELL None. **TASTE** Mild. Edible.
HABITAT Caespitose and gregarious upon the bark of living trees. Recorded by Cleland for SA. Description *ex* Lange & Hora. Attempts are being made to cultivate commercial strains in Australia.

Pluteus atromarginatus (Konrad) Kühn.

CAP To 6 cm; sooty-brown; darker at the centre; streaked with darker fibrils and the whole cap appearing fibrillose, but the fibrils closely adpressed; cuticle dry, peels.
FLESH White; thick, attenuated outwards.
GILLS White, then salmon-pink to pinky brown; free; crowded; margins finely dark brown or black; trama inverse; cystidia present.
STEM To 7 cm; pallid to brownish; solid; more or less bulbous at the base; dry; blackish or reddish-brown fibrils form a network over

the stem; no ring or volva; easily detached.

SPORES 7–7,5 x 5–6 μm; pink to salmon brown; sub-globose to more or less spherical or elliptical; smooth; basidia 4-spored.

SMELL None. **TASTE** Not recorded.

HABITAT On or very near dead wood, sometimes in troops or clusters.

WA

Pluteus cervinus (Schaeff. : Fr.) P. Kumm.

Almost identical to the preceding species except that the gills are not edged with black, and the spores are slightly larger, 7–8 x 5–6 μm; the stem fibrils are more evident and run as lines up and down the stem. Supposedly edible; Australian plants have yet to be tested.

HABITAT Solitary on wood, sawdust, stumps, etc.

WA SA

Psathyrella candolleanum (Fr.) Maire.

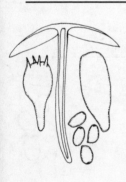

CAP To 4 cm; pallid, then pinkish brown at the margin and light ochre-brown at the centre; convex, then more or less planar, but remaining downturned at the margin; smooth; dry; margin often with velar fragments.

FLESH White; thin.

GILLS Pallid, then purplish grey; adnate; crowded; cystidia present.

STEM To 6 cm; white to slightly brownish; thin; brittle; hollow; no ring or volva.

SPORES 7–8 x 4.5–5.5 μm; grey-purple; smooth; elliptical; germ pore present; basidia 4-spored.

SMELL None. **TASTE** None.

HABITAT Near buried wood; on soil

amongst grass usually in troops or
clusters

NSW WA QLD

Psathyrella hydrophilum (Bull. ex Merat) Maire

CAP To 4 cm; date-brown drying pallid tan; hygrophanous; moist; uneven-
ly convex, then more or less plane;
margin striate or with small, white
velar fragments often remaining.

FLESH Concolorous with the cap;
watery; thin.

GILLS Pallid, then purplish brown;
more or less adnate, sometimes
adnexed or a little sinuate; crowded;
marginal cystidia present.

STEM To 5 cm; white; crisp; brittle; a
little flocculose on the surface; hollow; no ring or volva; occasionally a
zone of fibrils occurs at the veil site.

SPORES 5–9 x 3–5 μm; purple-black;
smooth; ellipsoid; germ pore present.

SMELL None. TASTE None.

HABITAT Densely tufted on buried
wood.

WA

Psilocybe subaeruginosa Clel.

CAP To 4 cm; olive-brown, often with
bluish patches; drying golden-
brown; more or less conical or
umbonate with a very pointed
umbo; margin may at first have a
few fragments of a pallid or whitish
veil.

POISONOUS

FLESH White; thin.

GILLS At first pallid grey-brown, then
in stages to inky-purplish; thin and
unequal; adnate to adnexed.

STEM To 10 cm; white or stained
dingy-grey in patches; streaked
bluish in the lower portion of the
stem, occasionally greenish; base

sometimes a little swollen; hollow or
stuffed; usually no traces of a ring,
but there may occasionally be very
faint traces in the immature stages.

SPORES 10–15 x 5–9 μm; oval; purplish black; smooth; basidia 4-
spored.

SMELL None. TASTE None or mealy.

Poisonous; hallucinogenic.

HABITAT Solitary or gregarious in
rank grass in wet eucalypt forest.

SA VIC NSW

Russula aff. *cyanoxantha* (Schaeff. ex Secr.) Fr.

CAP To 15 cm; purplish, brownish or
greenish, but generally with at least
some tinges of green—some reports
give greenish blotches on a greyish
background, but very variable; convex, then plane and a little depressed.

FLESH White, turns olive slowly with
ferrous sulphate; thick.

GILLS Whitish or very pale cream;
adnate; flexible with a faintly oily
feel.

STEM To 10 cm; white; sometimes
flushed purplish; firm; no ring or volva.

SPORES 7–9 x 6–7 μm; white; warty;
oval; amyloid; basidia 4-spored.

SMELL None. TASTE Mild.

HABITAT Amongst leaf litter in open
forest.

VIC

NOTE This Australian plant is probably a distinct species in its own
right; it is retained here for want of
further taxonomical studies.

Russula aff. *emetica* (Schaeff. : Fr.) S.F. Gray

CAP To 10 cm; bright scarlet to
cherry red; convex to plane; cuticle
peels exposing reddish flesh
beneath; more or less viscid then

dry; margin delicately striate.

FLESH White; thick; brittle; sphaerocysts present.

GILLS White, becoming creamy
white; adnate; crowded.

STEM To 8 cm; white; smooth; dry;
no ring or volva; cylindrical.

SPORES 9–11 x 7.5–8.5 μm; white or
creamy; warty; more or less
oval;amyloid; basidia 4-spored.

SMELL Faintly fruity. **TASTE** Very
acrid or hot. Will cause severe stomach upsets if eaten raw.

HABITAT On soil, woodland.

VIC NSW

Russula aff. *foetens* (Pers. : Fr.) Fr.

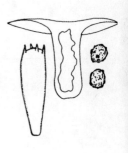

CAP To 10 cm; dingy brownish or
yellowish brown; more or less convex, but depressed in the centre; viscid, espesially in wet weather; margins tubercular striate.

FLESH White; thick; fragile.

GILLS Creamy white; adnate; crowded.

STEM To 5 cm; white with brownish
stains at the base; dry; no ring or
volva.

SPORES 7–9 μm; cream; sub-globose;
strongly warted; amyloid.

SMELL Strong; rubbery or of burnt
oil.

TASTE Intensely hot and peppery,
often appearing after about 10 to 15
seconds, and then very difficult to
assuage without rinsing the mouth
with water.

HABITAT Solitary or in twos and
threes on soil amongst forest litter.

NSW VIC QLD

NOTE This species is probably not
identical to the European plant, but
its closeness seems reasonably certain.

Russula aff. *fragilis* (Pers. : Fr.) Fr.

CAP   To 6 cm; reddish to purplish, rarely yellowish; convex to flattened, but usually delicate and fragile.

FLESH   White; thin.

GILLS   White to very pale cream; adnate; margins wavy and jagged under a hand lens.

STEM   To 6 cm; white, sometimes faintly yellow; more or less cylindrical; smooth; dry; no ring or volva.

SPORES   7.5–9 x 6–8 μm; white; more or less globose; warts more or less conical, amyloid; basidia 4-spored.

SMELL   Faintly of pears. TASTE   Very hot or acrid.

HABITAT   On soil amongst leaf litter in open forest.

NSW VIC

Russula lenkunya Grgurinovic

CAP   To 7 cm; purplish to red or wine-brown; more or less plane; a little moist when fresh; margin tubercular-striate; dry.

FLESH   Moderately thick.

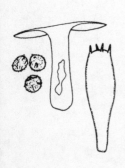

GILLS   White or very faintly creamy; adnate to adnexed; crowded.

STEM   To 5 cm; rosy pink; stout; cylindrical; brittle; smooth; solid then cavernous; no ring or volva.

SPORES   8.5–9 x 7–8 μm; white; more or less globose; apiculus prominent; decorated with amyloid warts; basidia 1, 2 or 4-spored.

SMELL   None. TASTE   Mild.

HABITAT   Solitary on soil in forest litter.

WA SA VIC NSW QLD

NOTE   This species is certainly not Peck's species which has a finely tomentose cap: Australian plants are smooth. Until further details are

known it is retained here for convenience. The species is common
and very distinctive.

Russula aff. *pectinatoides* Peck

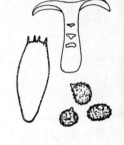

CAP To 10 cm; patchily dark biscuit
brown, paler towards the margin;
surface moist, sticky or slightly viscid; convex to depressed; margin
tubercular striate.
FLESH White; brittle; thick.
GILLS White; may discolour cream;
more or less adnate; crowded.
STEM To 6 cm; up to 3 cm thick;
white; discolouring brown; cavernous; dry; no ring or volva.
SPORES 6.5–8 x 5–6 μm; pale cream;
warts rounded, occasionally forming
reticulations; amyloid; basidia 4-
spored.
SMELL None. TASTE Mild.
HABITAT Solitary or in twos and
threes on soil amongst leaf litter in
open woodland or forest.
NOTE Cleland recorded this species
for SA and NSW; further collections
are needed to confirm the species.

Russula persanguinea Clel.

CAP To 8 cm; near blood-red; more
or less convex to plane; sometimes a
little depressed at the centre; cuticle
peels; margins tubercular striate.
FLESH White, slightly red under the
cuticle; thin.
GILLS White, later creamy; adnexed;
close.
STEM To 5 cm; white; stout; sometimes flattened; no ring or volva.
SPORES 7.5–11 x 7.5–9 μm; warty;
oval; amyloid; basidia 4-spored;
creamy white.

HABITAT   On soil amongst litter in open woodland.

SA

Russula purpureoflava Clel.

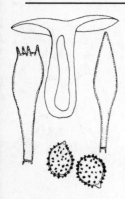

CAP   To 6 cm; purplish red to dark purplish brown; irregularly convex to plane or a little depressed at the centre; cuticle peels; surface slightly sticky; edges may be tubercular-striate.

FLESH   White with yellowish tinges; thin.

GILLS   Yellow; adnate; close; fusoid cheilocystidia present.

STEM   To 4 cm; all shades from pallid yellow with rosy tints to coral pink and yellowish at the base; slightly rough; dry; no ring or volva; solid, but may be cavernous.

SPORES   7.5–10 x 6.5–8.5 μm; yellowish white; sub-spherical; warts amyloid; basidia 4-spored.

SMELL   Slightly acidic   TASTE   Mild.

HABITAT   On soil amongst forest litter.

SA NSW QLD

Schizophyllum commune Fr.

CAP   To 8 cm; pale grey but may be greenish from algae in very old specimens; irregularly convex or fan-shaped; surface densely covered with short hairs at the point of attachment and finely velvety over the remainder; dry; margin lobed and often ragged, especially in old plants.

FLESH   White; thin, very tough.

GILLS   White to pallid grey or brownish; distant; radial from point of attachment; split longitudinally along the margins and each half curls over to protect the hymenium in dry weather.

STEM None or rudimentary.

SPORES 5.5–7 x 2.5–3.5 μm; white; smooth; oblong; iodine negative; basidia 4-spored.

SMELL None. TASTE Not recorded.

HABITAT Any dead wood; gregarious and often clustered; new caps sometimes appear on the under-surface of very old caps.

AUSTRALIA generally.

NOTE *Schizophyllum commune* is not really an agaric at all, despite the apparent gills. Intensive studies have shown that it belongs rather with the polyporoid genera; however, its macroscopic structure is such that it is usually looked for amongst the gilled fungi and so it is placed here for convenience.

Stropharia rugosoannulata Farlow

CAP To 8 cm; chestnut brown with reddish tints; convex; smooth; viscid in wet weather, greasy in dry weather; cuticle peels; margin usually with veil fragments.

FLESH White; thick.

GILLS Pallid; then greyish purple, finally black; margin pallid; adnate and ascending; crowded; cystidia present.

STEM To 9 cm; grey-fawn above the prominent ring, clay-pink below — there is often a red striate band just below the point of gill attachment; smooth; dry; hollow; stout; ring creamy white, double, the lower section toothed like a cog-wheel; basal rhizomorphs present; no volva.

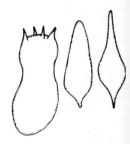

SPORES 12.5–13.5 x 8.5–9.5 μm; grey to blackish with a purple tint; germ pore present; smooth; elliptical; basidia 4-spored.

SMELL Strong and musty. TASTE Mild.
HABITAT In twos and threes in rich, well manured soil or old cow pats.

Stropharia semiglobata (Batsch : Fr.) Quel.

CAP To 4 cm; yellowish brown to yellow; hemispherical; viscid.
FLESH Whitish to pallid tan; thin.
GILLS Chocolate coloured; adnate.
STEM To 12 cm; white to yellowish brown; smooth; viscid below the ring; hollow; ring fixed; stained blackish from the spores; no volva.
SPORES 15–20 x 8–10 μm; violet-black; smooth; elliptical; with germ pore; basidia 4-spored.
SMELL None. TASTE None, or mealy.
HABITAT On manure in twos threes, or solitary.

VIC SA

Tricholoma aff. *acerbum* (Bull. : Fr.) Quel.

CAP To 9 cm; warm old gold; more or less convex; smooth to slightly fibrillose; margin at first inrolled; dry.
FLESH Golden yellow; thick.
GILLS Concolorous with the cap; minutely serrate edge; more or less sinuate; cystidia present.
STEM To 7 cm; concolorous with the cap; thick; hollow; smooth; dry; no ring or volva.
SPORES 7–8 x 6 μm; white; broadly elliptical; iodine negative; basidia 4-spored.
SMELL None. TASTE None.
HABITAT In sandy soil, open woodland.

WA VIC

Tricholoma nudum (Bull. : Fr.) P. Kumm. [= *Lepista nuda* (Bull.: Fr.) Cooke.]

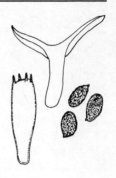

CAP To 10 cm; lilac to sooty lilac; dry; more or less convex to plane; smooth; margins more or less wavy.
FLESH Pale violet; thick.
GILLS Pale lilac; sinuate; crowded.
STEM To 8 cm; pale lilac to cap colour; slender to stout; solid; mealy; no ring or volva.
SPORES 6–8 x 4.5–5 μm; pale pinkish; minutely echinulate; iodine negative; ellipsoid; basidia 4-spored.
SMELL Floury. TASTE Pleasant. Edible.
HABITAT On soil or leaf litter under conifers or eucalypts.

SA VIC NSW

NOTE The pale pink, echinulate spores separates this species from *Tricholoma*, a genus with smooth, white spores.

Tricholoma aff. *rutilans* (Schaeff. : Fr.) P. Kumm. [= *Tricholomopsis rutilans* (Schaeff. : Fr.) Sing.]

CAP To 7.5 cm; reddish brown to purplish red, the colours caused by purplish red scales on a yellowish background; scaly; dry; convex to subumbonate; margins with short red hairs.

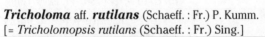

POISONOUS

FLESH Yellowish; thick.
GILLS Bright chrome yellow; thick; close; adnexed; edges serrate; rather waxy.
STEM To 5 cm; reddish brown to wine-brown; minutely velvety from tiny scales; stout; solid; no ring or volva.
SPORES 5–7 x 4.5–5 μm; white; sub-spherical; smooth.
SMELL None. TASTE Bitter.**Poisonous.**
HABITAT On stumps or wood; often in small clusters.

SA VIC QLD

Tricholoma sublilacinum Clel.
[= *Lepista sublilacina* (Clel.) Grgurinovic]

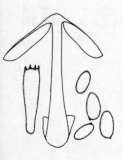

CAP   To 8 cm; grey-lilac, becoming greyish-white when dry; hydrophanous; convex but becoming irregular and repand when old; smooth; moist.

FLESH   White, tinted lilac; thick, watery; becoming white when dry.

GILLS   Grey-lilac; crowded; sinuate.

STEM   To 6 cm; concolorous with the cap; solid; dry; smooth; white fleshed; no ring or volva.

SPORES   5–6 x 3–4 μm; white; very finely verruculate; ellipsoid; iodine negative; basidia 4-spored.

SMELL   Strong; fungousy. TASTE   Mild.

HABITAT   Usually in circles on lawns and pastures, playing fields.

NSW VIC SA QLD

Volvaria speciosa (Fr. ex Fr.) Sing.

CAP   To 12 cm; pure white to sooty brown; at first spherical then convex and finally more or less plane, but usually with a small, central umbo; very viscid; cuticle peels; margin striate.

FLESH   Grey-white; very watery; thin.

GILLS   Pallid then pinkish, finally salmon-brown; free; crowded; margins minutely irregular under a hands lens.

STEM   To 20 cm; white to pallid tan; slender; hollow; smooth; delicately tomentose at the extreme base inside the volva; no ring; easily detached from the cap; volva white, bag-like, loose sheathing.

SPORES   15–17 x 9.5–10 μm; dull salmon-pink to brownish pink; smooth; elliptical; apiculus prominent; basidia 4-spored.

SMELL None. TASTE Mild. Originally considered poisonous, it was later found to be eaten regularly as a choice species in parts of Spain and North Africa. A closely allied species is the Oriental esculent, the `straw mushroom' *V. volvacea*. Australian plants have yet to be tested for edibility.

HABITAT Solitary, or in twos and threes on rich soil, particularly amongst tall weeds in waste land.

NSW VIC SA WA

NOTE The sooty-grey species is sometimes named *V. speciosa* var. *gloiocephala*. *Volvariella* is synonymous with *Volvaria*.

Volvaria aff. *taylori* (Berk. & Br.) Sing.

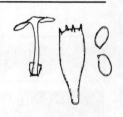

CAP To 2 cm; brown; a little scaly; dry; somewhat umbonate, radially fibrillose.

FLESH Very thin, white.

GILLS Free; salmon-pink.

STEM To 4 cm; thin; white; smooth; dry; no ring; volva white, friable, and leaving little or no traces on the cap, or may be fibrosely brownish.

SPORES 7–8.5 x 4.5–5.5 μm; salmon-pink; smooth; elliptical; hyaline under the microscope; basidia 4-spored.

SMELL None. TASTE Not recorded.

HABITAT Solitary on old dead stumps.

NSW

NOTE The species collected seems close to *V. taylori*, but, like so many of the Australian species, the similarity may be superficial and the above plant is possibly a new species that is distinct from the European species.

Xeromphalina tenuipes (Schw.) A.H. Sm.

CAP To 2 cm; rusty yellow-brown, darker towards the centre; more or less convex, becoming plane and then may be depressed at the centre; tough; striate when moist; smooth.

FLESH Concolorous with the cap; very thin.

GILLS Yellow; adnate; more or less distant; connected by veins on the under-surface.

STEM To 4 cm; date-brown; horny; polished; base strigose; no ring or volva.

SPORES 6.5–7.5 x 2.5–3.5 μm; white; oval; amyloid; smooth; basidia 4-spored.

SMELL None. TASTE Unknown.

HABITAT In troops on dead wood or bark.

NSW QLD

AGARICALES

BOLETACEAE

Boletellus emodensis (Berk.) Sing.

CAP To 6 cm; convex becoming more or less plane; heavily shaggy with pyramidal scales giving a pine-cone like effect, scale tips brown with the cuticle cracks between the scales bright crimson; velar remnants often found at the cap margins.

FLESH White; thick; becoming intense blue on cutting the cap, but pinkish in the stem.

PORES Old gold, but instantly turn blue on bruising or cutting, old pores become reddish and finally blackish; sulcate at the stem.

STEM To 8 cm; reddish near the pores, pale brown at the base, pallid above; solid; fibrillose; veil closely adpressed to stem; no volva.

SPORES 16.5–20 x 7.5–9 μm; brown; more or less fusiform or elongated elliptical; longitudinally striate.

SMELL Musty. TASTE Unknown.

HABITAT On rotting logs or stumps, especially in rainforest.

NSW VIC

NOTE There are a number of closely related species. Some variants of *B. emodensis* are almost completely pink.

Boletus cyanescens Bull. : Fr. [= *Gyroporus cyanescens* (Bull. : Fr.) Quel.]

CAP To 12 cm; light ochre; surface matt tomentose; convex; dry; often more or less contorted with age; turns blue-green when bruised.

FLESH White; thick; solid; turns blue-green instantly on cutting, but the colour slowly fades back from blue to white.

PORES White, then creamy, turn blue-green immediately on bruising; just reaching the stem; very small diameter; tubes easily removed from cap.

STEM To 10 cm; concolorous with cap; smooth; no ring or volva; becomes cavernous with age; bruises blue-green.

SPORES 9–10 x 6–7 μm; pale yellow; smooth; oval; basidia 4-spored.

SMELL Fruity. TASTE Mild.

HABITAT Usually solitary; on soil amidst eucalyptus litter.

WA

Boletus granulatus L. : Fr. [= *Suillus granulatus* (L. :Fr.) Kuntze.]

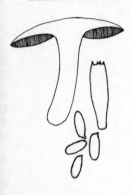

CAP To 15 cm; ochre-brown to yellow-brown; cuticle viscid to slimy and peeling readily; convex to irregular, plane or becoming a little repand.
FLESH Yellow-gold to pallid yellow; soft; thick; watery.
PORES At first bright yellow, finally old gold to olive brown; soft; readily detached from cap; at first weeping droplets of a clear or milky exudate, and dried droplets often encrust on the stem.
STEM To 8 cm; yellowish, a deeper yellow at the base; stout; solid; no ring or volva; encrusted or punctuate with blackish or brownish dots and markings which usually extend right down the stem.
SPORES 9.5–12 x 3.5–5 μm; brown; fusiform; apiculus prominent; smooth; basidia 4-spored.
SMELL Fruity. **TASTE** Mild, pleasant. Edible.
HABITAT Gregarious on soil amongst pine needles. Mycorrhizal on exotic pine species.
QLD NSW VIC SA WA

Boletus luteus L. : Fr. [= *Suillus luteus* (L. : Fr.) S.F. Gray.]

CAP To 8 cm; warm biscuit brown to olive or ochre-brown; cuticle very slimy and peeling; convex then plane.
FLESH Thick; soft; white, with yellowish tinges; watery.
PORES Yellow, becoming old gold with age; at first protected by a thick, white, more or less viscid veil which may become brown stained from the spores.
STEM To 10 cm; white; often a little

flocculose; thick; solid; the veil remaining as a thick, white, persistent, viscid ring; no volva.

SPORES 6.5–9.5 x 2.5–3.3 μm;

SMELL Fruity. TASTE Mild. Edible.

HABITAT Gregarious under introduced species of pine, on soil amongst needles etc.; mycorrhizal.

WA SA VIC NSW

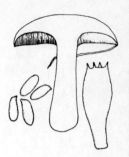

Boletus portentosus Berk. & Br. [= *Phaeogyroporus portentosus* (Berk. & Br.) McNabb.]

CAP To 100 cm; brown to yellowish, often with greenish tints; convex to uneven, margins often wavy; finely tomentose or scaly.

FLESH White with dirty grey tints, reddish around insect holes; very thick; firm and very difficult to cut.

PORES Pinkish yellow to yellowish green; dark brown when old or bruised, sometimes with reddish stains.

STEM To 20 cm; up to 10 cm diameter, occasionally more; dark dirty greenish brown, but darker at the base; very stout; thick; smooth to rough.

SPORES 7–8.5 x 5–6 μm.

SMELL Musty. TASTE Mild.

HABITAT Open or woodland areas; on soil sometimes in twos or threes.

WA SA NSW VIC QLD

Austroboletus cookei (Sacc. & Syd.) Singer

CAP To 15 cm; light orange to brown, darkening with age; convex to a little umbonate; very glutinous and slimy; margin with ragged veil fragments.

FLESH White; thick; very soft and soon riddled with insect holes.

PORES Light purple; very soft to

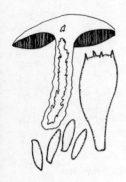

almost slimy in texture.

STEM To 12 cm; creamy white, but yellowish at the base and around the edges of the depressions and hollows of the lacunose surface; spongy; hollow; very slimy; no ring or volva; staining greenish where bruised.

SPORES 20–22 x 6–7 μm; brown; smooth; fusiform; basidia 4-spored.

SMELL Faintly fruity. **TASTE** Not recorded.

HABITAT In pine forest or eucalypt woodland; usually on rich soil with large quantities of humus; single, but usually common in any area where it is found.

WA NSW

'GASTEROMYCETES' OR SACK FUNGI

HYMENOGASTRALES

Rhizopogon rubescens Tul.

DESCRIPTION To 4 cm; rusty brown where exposed, but whitish to rosy pink or pinkish brown on soil-covered surfaces; turns pink where bruised; more or less round, elliptical or lobed; attached to the substrate by lateral, white rhizomorphs; gleba white, crisp, becoming brown, soft, spongy and watery when mature; sporophore rots to release the spores, it never becomes powdery.

SPORES 5.5–7 x 1.5–3.5 μm; hyaline or tinted; smooth; elliptical; septate.

HABITAT Semi-buried in soil or humus amongst the needles under introduced species of pine; mycorrhizal.

WA SA VIC NSW TAS

PHALLALES

Anthurus archeri (Berk.) Fisch.

DESCRIPTION To 12 cm; emerges from white, gelatinous 'egg'; stem length to 6 cm; white below, reddish orange above, spongy; arms numbering 4–8 and reddish orange to orange-red, united apically, but may separate in older plants, transversely rough on the inner surfaces where lies also the foetid smelling, olive-brown slimy spore-mass.

SPORES 6–7.5 x 2–5 μm; hyaline; smooth; elliptical; embedded in an olive-brown, foetid, mucilaginous slime.

SMELL Like sewage or rotten meat; very attractive to flies.

HABITAT Amongst forest litter on soil in open woodland.

NSW VIC TAS QLD

Aseroe rubra Labill. : Fr.

DESCRIPTION To 10 cm; emerges from a white, gelatinous 'egg', which may stain bluish on handling; the 'egg' splits to release a white, spongy stem up to 8 cm high; summit flattened, extending laterally into 4, 5 or 6 pairs of arms which are basally joined for the first 1 or 2 cm, colour bright red; central disc is perforated by a central hole and is covered by an olive-brown, slimy, foetid spore mass. Yellow, orange and pure white forms are known.

SPORES 5.5–6.5 x 2–3 μm; hyaline; smooth; cylindrical; embedded in a foetid, olive-brown mucilage.

SMELL Foetid, as of faeces or rotten meat.

HABITAT On rich soil; usually gregarious; in sheltered spots.

QLD NSW VIC TAS

Clathrus cibarius (Tul.) Fisch.

DETAILS Emerging from a white, more or less globose, gelatinous 'egg' up to 7 cm diameter; becomes a spherical, lattice work ball with occasionally a very rudimentary stem; white; readily detaches itself from the universal veil and is then blown about by the wind; gleba covers the inner surface of the lattice work and is olive-brown, slimy and foetid.

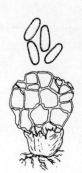

SPORES 4–6 x 1.5–2.5 μm; hyaline; smooth; more or less cylindrical; embedded in an olive-brown mucilage.

SMELL Foetid as of faeces or rotten meat.

HABITAT On soil amongst forest humus or litter, in small open spaces in woodlands, esp. beside forest tracks etc.

NSW VIC SA

NOTE See also *C. gracilis* which differs macroscopically in the colour of the spore mass.

Clathrus gracilis (Berk.) Schlechtendal

DETAILS Emerges from a dingy white, gelatinous 'egg' of up to 3 cm diameter to form a white, lattice work ball from 3 to 30 cm diameter; readily detached and blown about by the wind; gleba is sage-green, foetid, slimy and very copious — often dripping over the outside as well.

SPORES 4.5–6 x 1.5–2.5 μm; hyaline; smooth; cylindrical; embedded in a foetid, sage-green mucilage.

SMELL Foetid, as of faeces or rotten meat.

HABITAT In woodland open spaces, especially clearings or tracks.

WA NSW VIC SA QLD

NOTE See also *C. cibarius* which differs macroscopically only in the colour of the gleba. The lattice work arms are also of different internal construction in the two species; in *C. gracilis* the arms are seen to consist of two distinct tubes in cross-section, in *C. cibarius* the structure is merely cellular. *C. gracilis* is the more common of the two.

Clathrus pusillus Berk.

DESCRIPTION Emerges from a dingy-white gelatinous 'egg' up to 2 cm diameter; the lattice work ball is up to 4 cm diameter and bright red; gleba is olive-brown, foetid, slimy and covers the inner surface.

SPORES 4.5–5.5 x 1.5–2 μm; hyaline; smooth; cylindrical.

HABITAT On soil amongst grass.

WA VIC NSW QLD

NOTE It is possible that this species may be confused with *Colus hirudinosus*, however the stem in *Clathrus pusillus* is never so pronounced, nor are the arms so distinct.

Colus hirudinosus Cavalier & Sechier

DESCRIPTION Emerges from a whitish, gelatinous 'egg' of up to 3 cm diameter; sporophore height up to 7 cm; about 5 to 7 arms are attached basally to a short hollow stem which is more or less whitish to pinkish and mostly hidden by the volva; the arms are bright red and unite apically to form a small lattice work at the very summit; the gleba is olive-brown and covers the inside of the upper lattice and arms.

SPORES 5–6 x 1.5–2 μm; hyaline; elliptical; smooth; embedded in a foetid, olive-brown mucilage.

SMELL Foetid, as of faeces or rotten meat.

HABITAT On soil amongst forest humus.

NSW SA QLD

NOTE It is possible to confuse this species with *Clathrus pusillus*, but *C. pusillus* never has such a pronounced stem, nor the very distinct arms.

Dictyophora indusiata (Vent.) Desv.

DESCRIPTION To 20 cm; emerges from a white or pallid pink, gelatinous 'egg' of up to 4 cm diameter; expands to form a spongy, white stem up to 18 cm high, with a conical white cap at the summit up to 3 cm high; the cap has a reticulate surface which is covered by the olive-brown, foetid spore mass; the 'egg' remains as a volva; a white, lacy veil (the indusium), extends from under the cap to nearly touching the ground (may later shrink somewhat in size).

SPORES 3.5–4.5 x 1.5–2 μm; hyaline; smooth; cylindrical; embedded in an olive-brown, foetid mucilage.

SMELL Foetid as of faeces or rotten meat.

HABITAT On rich soil in sheltered spots.

QLD NSW

Dictyophora multicolor Berk. & Br.

DESCRIPTION To 16 cm; emerges from a white, violet or brownish tinted 'egg' which may occasionally be covered with short, soft, brownish spines; basal rhizomorphs may be tinted pallid violet; expanding to a spongy white, pink or orange stem of up to 16 cm height, topped by a conical orange cap, the surface of which is reticulate and is covered with the olive-brown, slimy, extremely foetid gleba; a salmon-pink to orange-red lacy veil (indusium) extends from under the cap to almost the ground, but may later shrink in size somewhat; the 'egg' remnants remain as a volva.

SPORES 3.5–4.5 x 1.5–2 μm; tinted; smooth; cylindrical; embedded in an olive-brown, very foetid mucilage.

SMELL Extremely foetid.

HABITAT Sheltered, moist positions in rich soil especially rainforest; can appear in the same position year after year; often gregarious.

QLD NSW VIC

Lysurus gardneri Berk.

DESCRIPTION To 12 cm; unexpanded 'eggs' to 3 cm; 'eggs' dingy white, splitting open to release a white creamy white or pinkish spongy stem which expands rapidly upwards; at the summit are typically 5 to 7 arms which project vertically upwards, are narrower at their free ends and are pallid orange to rose red; gleba is brown, foetid and slimy and lies on the inner surface of the arms.

SPORES 4.5–5 x 1.5–2 μm; hyaline; smooth; elliptical; embedded in an brown, foetid, mucilage.

SMELL Foetid, as of faeces or rotten meat.

HABITAT On humus-rich soils.

QLD NSW

Lysurus mokusin L. ex Fr.

DESCRIPTION To 15 cm; emerges from a white, globose, gelatinous 'egg' about 3 cm diameter; the 'egg' splits open to release a more or less white, fluted, many angled stem which narrows towards the base; the summit bears typically 4 to 6 arms up to 3 cm long which are roughened and orange; the foetid, olive-brown spore mass is borne on the interior surfaces of the arms.

SPORES 4–5 x 1.5–2.5 μm; hyaline, but noted as tinted by Cunningham; elliptical; smooth; embedded in an olive-brown, foetid mucilage.

SMELL Foetid as of faeces or rotten meat.

HABITAT On humus-rich soils; sheltered positions.

QLD NSW

Phallus hadriani Pers. ex Vent.

DESCRIPTION To 10 cm; emerges from a whitish to rather pinkish, gelatinous 'egg' which rapidly stains more or less violet where bruised; the 'egg' splits open to release a white, cylindrical, spongy stem about 10 cm high, which carries a white cap at the summit; the cap is conical and has a white, reticulated surface which is coated with an olive-brown to olive-green, highly foetid slime; white rhizomorphs are frequently found at the base of the 'egg'

SPORES 3–5 x 2–2.5 μm; hyaline; smooth; cylindrical; embedded in an olive-brown, foetid mucilage.

SMELL Very foetid, of faeces or an open sewer.

HABITAT Gregarious on humus rich, sandy soil under shrubs or trees.

WA

NOTE The species is very close to the European *P. impudicus*, but differs in the distinct violet tints which appears on the pinkish 'egg' when it is bruised. So far it has been noted only from King's Park in WA.

Phallus rubicundus (Bosc.) Fr.

DESCRIPTION To 15 cm; emerging from a white, gelatinous 'egg' about 3 cm diameter; the 'egg' splits open to release a spongy, scarlet or orange stem which carries a scarlet, or orange, conical cap at the summit; the top is often perforate; the cap surface is usually a little rough and carries on it the olive-brown, foetid, spore-bearing slime.

SPORES 3.5–5 x 1.5–2 μm; hyaline to tinted; smooth; cylindrical; embedded in an olive-brown foetid mucilage produced by the collapse of the glebal tissues.

SMELL Foetid, as of faeces or rotten meat.

HABITAT Amongst rich soil and plant debris in forests.

QLD NSW VIC SA TAS

SCLERODERMATALES

Pisolithus marmoratus (Berk.) Fischer

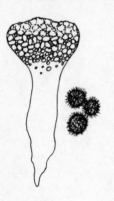

DESCRIPTION To 15 cm high; the peridium up to 5 cm diameter; more or less a dirty, whitish grey when immature and looks as if a thin, white membrane has been placed over the peridium and then been perforated by match-head sized holes; soon becomes dull to shiny black; the more or less globular peridium becomes very brittle when mature, and the peridial wall crumbles away to release the powdery spores.

GLEBA At first white, then ochre or pinkish, finally purplish brown to chocolate brown; enclosed in rice-grain-shaped capsules about 2 to 3 mm diameter which crumble away when mature to release the spores. Specific gravity very light.

SPORES 8–9 μm; brown; globose; echinulate; purplish brown to chocolate brown.

HABITAT On soil, usually near eucalypts, with which is mycorrhizal; usually gregarious, and sometimes caespitose, sometimes the glebas become interconnected when caespitose plants fuse their peridia.

WA SA VIC NSW QLD TAS NT

Pisolithus aff. *tinctorius* (Mich. ex Pers.) Ckr. & Couch

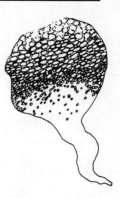

DESCRIPTION To 10 cm; peridium globular, attached to a long, orange-yellow, rooting base; very robust and feel heavy like a piece of lead in the hand; peridium white or ochre-brown, but becomes tarry black where bruised; peridium fragments in small, leathery pieces as the gleba matures; stains objects bright yellow as they touch it or the blackish, mucilaginous juice.

GLEBA At first white, it becomes yellow ochre, and powdery; composed of rice-grain-like packages that can readily be pulled free of the general context; the spores are released by the slow integration from the summit downwards of the peridial wall and the 'rice-grains', or tramal plates as they are more correctly called. Specific gravity quite heavy.

SPORES 8–12 μm; yellowish; globose; echinulate.

HABITAT Gregarious amongst leaf litter in sandy soils.

WA NSW VIC QLD

NOTE This species has a dye present; see earlier section on the uses of fungi.

Scleroderma australe Mass.

DESCRIPTION To 5 cm; pallid straw-yellow to bright yellow; more or less globular or lobed; the base is formed by a series of rhizomorphs which may coalesce to form a short stem; usually the plant is directly on the ground; smooth to scaly or finely cracked; the tough peridial wall ruptures to release the spores, and may form a stellate cup that is bright yellow; the peridial wall is tough and leathery.

GLEBA White, then more or less violet (often dark), finally brown; becoming dry and powdery.

SPORES 6–8.5 μm; brown; globose; echinulate.

HABITAT On soil amongst forest litter.

WA NSW SA VIC QLD

Scleroderma verrucosum Vaill. ex Pers.

DESCRIPTION To 4 cm; yellowish to ochre; more or less globose; the base is stem-like and rooting; peridium covered in small, scaly warts; occasionally an irregularly torn stoma is produced.

GLEBA At first white, then olive, finally brown and powdery.

SPORES 10–12 μm; brown; globose; echinulate.

HABITAT On sandy soil amongst leaf litter.

NSW SA

LYCOPERDALES

Calvatia caelatum (Bull.) Morg.

DESCRIPTION To 8 cm; white, then pallid brown; more or less globose with a prominent sterile base; outer layer cracks irregularly then forms a mosaic pattern; base quite thick, separated from the spore mass by a

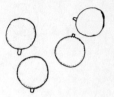

diaphragm; the outer wall breaks away irregularly to release the dry, dusty spore mass; finally only the sterile base may be left.

GLEBA White, then brown, finally dry, dusty, powdery brown; never with tints of violet.

SPORES 3–5 μm; brown; globular; smooth with a pedicel stump.

HABITAT Solitary or a few together; in grassy areas.

NZ

NOTE It is not certain if this species occurs in Australia. The very similar *Calvatia lilacina* is often confused with *C. caelatum*, but the gleba is a distinct violet or lilac-brown when mature and is impossible to mistake. Description *ex* Cunningham.

Calvatia candida (Rostk.) Hollos.

DESCRIPTION To 6 cm; white, becoming pallid brown; globular to top-shaped; furfuraceous, the particles disappearing as the plant matures, whilst the peridium becomes very thin and papery; sterile base very well developed but there is no diaphragm; spores are released by irregular fracture and breakdown of the peridial wall; gleba white, then olive-brown, dry and powdery.

SPORES 4–5 μm; brown; globose; echinulate; pedicellate.

HABITAT On soil amongst grass; often gregarious.

NSW VIC SA WA NT

Calvatia gigantea (Batsch ex Pers.) Lloyd

DESCRIPTION To 40 cm; creamy white to white; more or less globose to elliptical; exterior dry, often finely tomentose; peridial wall leathery;

base rather scanty or absent; no diaphragm; gleba white, then yellowish, finally olive-brown and powdery; released as the peridial wall disintegrates.

SPORES 4–6 μm; brown; globose; pedicellate; delicately verrucose.

TASTE Edible when gleba is still white.

HABITAT Singly in pastures.

SA NSW

Calvatia lilacina (Berk.) P. Henn.

DESCRIPTION To 10 cm; creamy white to brown; more or less globose with a prominent rooting base; exterior smooth or flaky, cracking into an irregular mosaic; the well developed sterile base is separated from the gleba by a distinct diaphragm; gleba powdery at maturity and released as the exterior crumbles away irregularly from the top, often leaving only the sterile base; gleba at first white, then brownish but always with a distinct lilac, violet or purplish tint, finally more or less lilac-brown.

SPORES 5–7.5 μm; globose; pedicellate; irregularly warty; brown under the microscope.

TASTE Edible whilst the gleba is still white.

HABITAT On soil, sometimes gregarious or even forming rings; amongst grass or plant litter.

SA VIC NSW QLD

NOTE This species is very similar to *C. caelatum*, but *Calvatia caelatum* has no lilac tints at all in the spore mass.

Geastrum fenestriatum (Pers.) Fisch.

DESCRIPTION To 4 cm; globose and more or less buried; the peridial layers then split into 4 or 5 rays, which arch strongly upwards and remain attached to the mycelial base only at the extreme tips; the inner peridial wall remains globose and stands on a short stem at the top of the arched star; inner peridial wall rusty to dark brown and finely pubescent, more or less 3 cm diameter; there is a single, tubular stoma through which the rusty-brown, dry, powdery spore mass can escape.

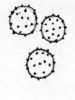

SPORES 4–5 μm; rusty brown; globose; verrucose.

HABITAT Amongst leaf litter under trees.

VIC SA WA

Geastrum limbatum Fr.

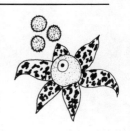

DESCRIPTION To 7 cm diameter across the rays; the outer peridial wall splits stellately to give 6 to 9 rays, which are sepia to rusty brown but become pallid in irregular patches so the effect is somewhat blotchy; the lower ray surfaces are dirt encrusted; inner peridial wall remains globose, grey and is whitely flocculose, the particles rubbing off to leave a papery wall; stoma is distinct and surrounded by a well-marked circular, slightly depressed area, the peristome; gleba brown, dry, powdery.

SPORES 4.5–5 μm; brown; echinulate; globular.

HABITAT Gregarious on soil under shrubs; usually half-buried.

NSW

Geastrum triplex Jungh.

DESCRIPTION To 12 cm across the rays; outer peridial wall splitting into 5 to 8 more or less brown rays; the middle peridial wall persists as a collar at the base of the central globose sack; the inner peridial sack is light brown and smooth; the stoma is very definite and surrounded by a small circular marking (the peristome); gleba brown, dry, powdery — often rusty brown.

SPORES 4–5.5 μm; rusty brown; more or less globose; irregularly verrucose.

HABITAT Gregarious amongst leaf litter under trees.

NSW SA VIC WA TAS QLD

Lycoperdon perlatum Pers.

DESCRIPTION To 5 cm; yellowish becoming dirty brown; more or less globose, tapering into a more or less cylindrical stem; peridium covered in small, white, pointed granules which slowly disappear to leave a papery, bay-brown sack with a definite stoma; sterile base very prominent; no diaphragm; gleba yellowish, then olive-brown.

SPORES 4–6 μm; brown; globose; echinulate.

HABITAT Amongst humus in woods.

NSW TAS

Lycoperdon pyriforme Schaeff. ex Pers.

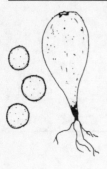

DESCRIPTION To 5 cm; grey to brownish; more or less globose, tapering gradually into a sterile base; diaphragm absent; at first covered with tiny granules and pointed warts scattered over the surface like sand grains, but these soon disappear; stoma rather torn; gleba greenish yellow, then olive or rusty brown.

SPORES 3.5–4.5 μm; brown; delicately rough to almost smooth; globose.

HABITAT Caespitose to gregarious on rotting wood; rhizomorphs present.

QLD NSW VIC SA

Myriostoma coliforme Corda

DESCRIPTION To 8 cm; grey-brown to cinnamon brown, splitting into 5 to 10 rays; the central globose peridium is supported on several small stem-like structures scattered irregularly under the central peridial ball; the central sack is of a grey colour and the spore mass escapes by means of one to several small torn mouths; as many as fifteen mouths have been counted, the effect rather like a pepper-pot; gleba brown, dry, powdery.

SPORES 4–6 μm; globose; verrucose to somewhat echinulate, the spines rather blunt; brown.

HABITAT On leaf mould under trees; solitary; introduced.

NSW

Podaxis pistillaris (L. ex Pers.) Fr.

DESCRIPTION To 15 cm; more or less white to pallid brown; smooth to scaly; shaped like an elongated drumstick, the head about 5 cm long or a little more; peridium attached to the stem at the summit and closely adpressed to the stem; opening at the base to release the spores, then sometimes detaching from the summit and splitting, finally removed by the wind to leave the powdery spore mass exposed on the top and sides of the stem; stem solid, woody, twisted and cracking longitudinally; gleba powdery, reddish brown to black.

SPORES 13–14 x 12 μm; black; smooth; thick walled; with germ pore.

HABITAT Solitary or gregarious in dry to very dry regions, on sandy or clay soil. (The author's own collections are from Kalgoorlie in WA.)

WA QLD SA NT NSW

Tulostoma albicans White ex Cunn.

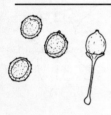

DESCRIPTION To 1 cm; dingy white; outer layer rapidly vanishes leaving a collar at the base; inner peridial layer thin and papery, globose, and with a distinct tubular stoma; stem up to 2.5 cm, finely striate, a little bulbous at the base, dingy white.

GLEBA Brown, dry, powdery.

SPORES 4.5–5.5 (6) μm; brown; globose; finely verrucose.

HABITAT In soil with only the globose peridium showing above ground.

WA SA NT NSW VIC TAS

Tulostoma obesum Cke. & Ell. ex Cunn.

DESCRIPTION To 1 cm; dingy white; smooth; papery; middle peridial layer persists as a basal collar around the globose peridial sack remaining; stoma torn and fibrillose; stem up to 2.5 cm, brownish, longitudinally striate and slightly bulbous.

SPORES 4–6 μm; rusty brown; smooth; globose.

HABITAT Single or gregarious on soil; the stem is completely buried so that the plant appears rather like a normal puff-ball.

NSW VIC SA WA NT

NIDULARIALES

Crucibulum vulgare Tul.

DESCRIPTION To 1.5 cm; more or less cup-shaped; bright cinnamon brown exteriorly, the interior pallid cinnamon; exterior silky smooth; interior smooth, shiny and containing small, flattened, bean-shaped objects (peridioles) of 1 to 2 mm diameter; the cup at first closed by a thin membrane, the epiphragm.

SPORES 7–10 x 4.5–5 μm; hyaline; elliptical; smooth; contained in the peridioles.

HABITAT Gregarious upon dead twigs or plant litter.

NSW VIC SA WA TAS

Cyathus stercoreus (Schwein.) de Toni

DESCRIPTION To 1 cm; cup funnel-shaped; exterior cinnamon brown and shaggy tomentose, sometimes rather matted; interior blackish brown and quite smooth; containing large numbers of olive-brown to black lens-shaped objects (peridioles), each about 1 to 2 mm diameter.

SPORES 20–40 μm; smooth; hyaline; ovoid; contained in the peridioles.

HABITAT Gregarious on dung.

QLD NSW VIC SA WA

Nidula candida (Peck) White

DESCRIPTION To 15 mm; white becoming dingy brown; cup-shaped; exterior shaggy; interior smooth and shining and containing numbers of lens-shaped objects (peridioles) reddish brown in colour, 1 to 2 mm diameter.

SPORES 6–9 x 4–5.5 μm; hyaline;

smooth; elliptical; produced within the peridioles.

HABITAT Solitary or gregarious on dead sticks.

NOTE This species is known from New Zealand, but not so far from Australia. It resembles an Australian species called *N. emodensis* which is a little smaller, is finely tomentose rather than shaggy, and has a brown interior to the cup rather than the white or yellow tinted interior of the species *N. candida*. Description *ex* Cunningham.

ASCOMYCOTINA

PYRENOMYCETES

CLAVICIPITALES

Cordyceps gunnii (Berk.) Berk.

DESCRIPTION To 12 cm; deep olive-green with brownish tinges grading into yellow on the stem, the underground portion of which is white; the olive-green head is about 5 to 6 cm long, more or less smooth, or with very shallow, longitudinal grooves; perithecia almost invisible and observed only with a hand lens; club-shaped, the head rather elongated like a cigar.

SPORES Extremely difficult to obtain whole, as they break into smaller sections; the sections are hyaline, smooth and 5–8 μm; whole spores are extremely long and thin.

HABITAT On very large caterpillars which pupate buried in the soil, the caterpillars usually up to 7 or 8 cm long. In woodland or forest, apparently on soil.

QLD NSW VIC TAS SA

Cordyceps militaris (Fr.) Link

DESCRIPTION To 3 cm; orange; a simple club shape, sometimes flattened; the summit is fertile; perithecia prominent and appear as small, orange pimples scattered over the surface.

SPORES 3.5–6 x 1–1.5 μm; smooth; hyaline; fragmenting into smaller pieces.

HABITAT Often apparently on soil, but in fact springing from an insect chrysalis or a mummified caterpillar; often more than one orange stroma will be present on large insect hosts.
NSW VIC

Cordyceps taylori (Berk.) Sacc.

DESCRIPTION To 20 cm; shape similar to a deer antler; bay-brown to dark brown with blackish dots scattered all over the surface; perithecia prominent and appearing as small pimples on the surface of the coralloid stroma, but not over the ends of the branches; stipe brown and tomentose at the base; the host caterpillars are very large and they are usually about 2 cm thick and about 10 cm long.
HABITAT On large caterpillars buried in the soil, so that only the coralloid stroma appears above the ground; often in rainforest.
NSW VIC
Description *ex* Willis.

SPHAERIALES

Poronia erici Lohmayer & Benkert

DESCRIPTION To 1.5 cm; top-shaped or disc-like; the upper flattened surface white, with tiny black holes (ostioles) scattered over it; most of the plant is sunk into the substrate.
SPORES 22–34 x 14–18 μm; more or less bean shaped; hyaline; smooth.
HABITAT Always on dung. Differs from *P. punctata* by the much larger spores. The jet black *Poronia oedipus* Mont. may be found on old cow dung in Queensland.
WA SA VIC TAS

Xylaria aff. *polymorpha* (Pers. ex Merat) Dumortier

DESCRIPTION To 6 cm; irregularly club-shaped, and looking like distorted fingers; coal black; perithecial tops showing as even darker black pimples and quite prominent; flesh white, tough.

SPORES 18–30 x 5–8 μm; black; smooth; fusiform.

HABITAT Gregarious on tree stumps and logs.

NOTE Cooke records this species from both Queensland and New South Wales. The author has collected what may have been this species from rainforest in the Lamington Plateau area, southern Queensland, but the collection has unfortunately been destroyed. An apparently similar collection has been obtained from northern NSW but is sterile.

NSW QLD

DISCOMYCETES

PEZIZALES

Cheilymenia coprinaria (Cooke) Boud.

DESCRIPTION To 1 cm; cup-shaped, becoming flattened and discoid with a fringe of more or less brownish-black, short hairs on the edge or outer surface; disc may contort a little at maturity; at first translucent yellow, then brownish, reddish orange.

HYMENIUM Asci more or less cylindrical; 8-spored; iodine negative; paraphyses club-shaped and staining violet in iodine.

SPORES 16.5–18 x 9.5–10 μm; smooth,

elliptical; hyaline.

HABITAT Gregarious on old cow manure.

WA SA VIC TAS QLD

Morchella elata Fr.

DESCRIPTION To 10 cm; cap more or less conical, dark brownish olive, the ribs more or less longitudinal and irregularly connected by cross-ribs to produce vertical lines of pits, the pits are up to 1 cm wide, yellowish brown within and smoky-brown to black at the margins.

STEM To 5 cm; hollow; cylindrical, broader at the base; white to yellowish; surface somewhat mealy.

SPORES 20–24 x 12–14 μm; elliptical; smooth; septate; yellowish in mass; asci 8-spored.

HABITAT Open grounds in woods, often after fires; uncommon.

VIC SA QLD

NOTE All *Morchella spp.* seem to be uncommon in Australia.

Peziza aurantia Pers. ex Hook. [= *Aleuria aurantia* (Pers. : Fr.) Fuckel.]

DESCRIPTION To 7 cm; cupulate, then discoid, finally contorted; bright orange; smooth; mealy-downy exteriorly; seated directly on the ground.

HYMENIUM Smooth; asci 8-spored; paraphyses simple and club-shaped, septate.

SPORES 14–16 x 7–9 μm; hyaline; elliptical; reticulate.

HABITAT Gregarious directly on soil, either sandy or clay.

NSW VIC SA

Peziza scuttelata (L. ex St. Amans) Lamb

DESCRIPTION To 1 cm; discoid to irregular; margins fringed with brownish, stiff hairs; orange red to red; directly on the substrate.

SPORES 16–18 x 10–15 μm; hyaline; ellipsoid; smooth, then ornamented with tiny warts; asci 8-spored.

HABITAT Gregarious upon rotten wood, bark, or on the ground; occasionally on rotting leaves, wood ashes, or even the rotting caps of bracket fungi, but *never* on manure.

VIC SA WA

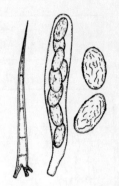

Peziza vesiculosa Bull. ex St. Amans

DESCRIPTION To 8 cm; light yellowish brown, darker inside; discoid, then more or less cupulate, finally contorted and the margins inrolling; exterior mealy and appearing as if there are vesicles around the rim of the cup.

SPORES 20–25 x 10–13 μm; hyaline; elliptical; smooth; asci cylindrical, 8-spored, deep blue in iodine; paraphyses simple, club-shaped and septate.

HABITAT Gregarious or clustered on manure, or sometimes upon very heavily manured soil; occasionally distorting because of mutual pressure.

QLD NSW VIC TAS SA WA

Plectania campylosporus (Berk.) Nannf. apud Korf.

DESCRIPTION To 5 cm; very dark sepia to almost black; cup-shaped to discoid, with a definite stem of up to 1 cm; looks and feels rubbery; exterior often mealy; cup margins minutely and delicately rough.

SPORES 23–32 x 9–14 μm; hyaline; smooth; bean-shaped; large oil globules present; asci 8-spored; paraphyses very slender.

HABITAT Gregarious on rotting wood.

NSW QLD VIC WA

HELOTIALES

Chlorosplenium aff. *aeruginascens* (Nyl.) Karst.

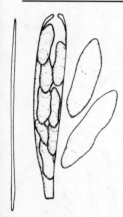

DESCRIPTION To 0.5 cm; more or less discoid on small, greenish black, 3 mm stems; the discs wholly green, but whitening with age; smooth.

ASCI Cylindrical; 8-spored; pored at the tip which also stains blue in Melzer's Iodine.

SPORES 6–10 x 1.5–2 μm; fusiform; hyaline; smooth.

HABITAT Gregarious on dead wood which is stained green by the mycelium.

NOTE *Chlorosplenium sp.* has been collected in Australia, especially from Queensland. However, they seem to be different from the above species; it is quite probable that we have a distinct species, and that all our plants should simply be labelled *Chlorosplenium sp.* until a true assessment has been made.

Trichoglossum walteri (Berk.) Durand

DESCRIPTION To 4.5 cm; black; club-shaped, but the read rather flattened; the stem is cylindrical and about 2 mm thick; the entire fungus is very finely velvety.

HYMENIUM Covers the entire club-head; paraphyses club-shaped at the tip and curling over like a shepherd's crook, not affected by Melzer's Iodine; asci hyaline, blue tipped in Melzer's Iodine, 8-spored, cylindrical; setae lanceolate, dark brown to black under the microscope.

SPORES 80–90 x 5–5.5 μm; brown when mature; cylindrical, rounded at the ends, often a little curved; at first without any septa, then becoming 3-septate and finally 7-septate.

HABITAT Gregarious, directly upon soil.

NSW

MYXOMYCOTINA

Fuligo septica Gmelin

DESCRIPTION Size very variable, 1 to 15 cm; pallid yellow to bright yellow, but sometimes whitish; often resembles an egg; old specimens become greyish white with a violet tint from the inner spore mass; often with a small whitish trail left behind it; texture brittle or friable.

SPORES 6–9 μm; violet; spherical; finely punctate.

HABITAT On wet grass, dead wood, leaves, etc.; solitary or gregarious; occasionally very wet seasons produce huge numbers on pastures.

QLD NSW VIC SA

GLOSSARY

adnate the gills are attached to the stem for their total width.

adnexed the gills just reach the stem.

adpressed closely flattened onto.

amyloid exhibit a blue-black reaction in Melzer's Iodine.

annulus ring of tissue found on the stem of some fungi.

ascocarp the fruiting body of an ascomycete.

ascus the spore-producing cell of an ascomycete.

basidium the spore-producing cell of a basidiomycete.

campanulate bell-shaped.

capillitium hyphal threads present in glebas of the puff-ball family.

coprophilous dung inhabiting.

coriaceous leathery.

cortina a cobweb-like veil found in certain toadstools.

cystidia specially shaped cells often observed on the gills of agarics.

decurrent the gills run for some distance down the stem.

dextrinoid exhibit a brick-red reaction in Melzer's Iodine.

echinulate spiny.

excentric offset to one side.

floccose covered in loose, small, cottony scales.

free the gills do not reach the stem.

fusiform spindle-shaped.

gleba spore-bearing tissue; especially in puff-ball family.

gregarious growing together in a small area; but separately, not caespitose.

habitat the environment of a fruiting body.

hispid covered with stiff, short hairs.

hygrophanous water-soaked and translucent, drying opaque.

hirsute hairy.

hymenium the exposed spore bearing tissues in the agarics.

hyphae the thread-like cells of a fungal mycelium.

infundibuliform funnel-shaped.

lacunose a surface with wide, sunken pits like an irregular honeycomb.

latex the fluid that may ooze from cut surfaces in some species.

marginate the basal bulb of a stem has a small circular ridge on its upper surface where a universal veil was attached.

mycelium the food absorbing hyphal mass.

mycology the study of fungi.

mycorrhiza a fungal –plant root association, probably symbiotic.

nodulose a surface with warty, blunted protuberances, especially spores.

parasite an organism that needs living tissues as its habitat.

pedicel a stem; especially the short stem on many puff-ball spores.

peridium the outer wall of a fungus; especially of puff-balls.

perithecium the sack-like fruiting bodies of certain ascomycetes.

pileus a cap; especially in the agarics.

plane flat; especially of caps in the agarics.

plicate folded or deeply striate; especially of caps in the agarics.

pruinose covered with a bloom, rather like chalk-dust.

pubescent covered with very fine, short, soft hairs.

punctate finely rough, as with minute pin-pricks.

repand upturned, especially of caps in the agarics.

rhizomorph a mycelial strand composed of many hyphae close together.

rimose splitting radially.

saprophyte an organism that requires dead tissues as its substrate.

sclerotium a hyphal mass generally used as a resting stage in some species.

septate divided by cross-walls; especially in spores or hyphae.

serrate saw-toothed; especially of gill margins.

sessile attached directly to the substrate.

sinuate notched; especially of gills which upturn just before the stem is reached.

sporophore the fungal fruiting body.

stellate star-shaped.

sterigma the stem at the summit of a basidium to which a spore is attached.

stipe the stem or stalk.

striate streaked with lines.

strigose covered with long, coarse hairs.

stroma a hard hyphal mass found in certain ascomycete species in which the perithecia are embedded.

substrate the layer upon which an organism is growing.

tomentose woolly; or thickly downy with soft, matted hairs.

umbo the central swelling of an otherwise plane cap.

universal veil an outer membrane that at first entirely covers the fungus.

veil a thin membrane, especially that covering the immature gills in agarics.

verrucose finely warty or rough; especially of spores.

viscid sticky or slimy.

volva the sack-like remnant of the universal veil found at the stipe base in certain species.

FURTHER READING

Aberdeen J.E.C. (1979) *Introduction to the Mushrooms, Toadstools and Larger Fungi of Queensland* Qld Naturalists Club Brisbane

Bougher N.L. and Syme Katrina (1998) *Fungi of Southern Australia* UWA Press, Perth.

Cleland J.B. (1934) *Toadstools and Mushrooms and other Larger Fungi of South Australia Vols I and II* Government Printer Adelaide

Cole M.F., Fuhrer B.A. and Holland A.A. (1978) *A Field Guide to the Common Genera of Gilled Fungi in Australia* Inkata Press Melbourne

Cooke M.C. (1892) *Handbook of Australian Fungi* Williams & Norgate London

Cunningham G.H. (1942) *The Gasteromycetes of Australia and New Zealand* John McIndoe Dunedin NZ

Findlay W.P.K. (1978) *The Observers Book of Mushrooms, Toadstools and other Common Fungi* Frederick Warne London

Fuhrer B. and Robinson R. (1992) *Rainforest Fungi of Tasmania and South-East Australia* CSIRO, Tasmanian Forestry Commission

Fuhrer B. (1985) *A Field Companion to Australian Fungi* Five Mile Press Hawthorne

Griffiths Kevn (1985) *A Field Guide to the Larger Fungi of the Darling Scarp and South West of Western Australia* Kevn Griffiths Perth

Macdonald R. and Westerman J. (1979) *A Field Guide to Fungi of South-eastern Australia* Thomas Nelson Melbourne

Phillips Roger (1981) *Mushrooms and other fungi of Great Britain and Europe* Ward Lock Limited London

Ramsbottom J. (1979) *Mushrooms and Toadstools* Collins London

Shepherd C.J. & Totterdell C.J. (1988) *Mushrooms and Toadstools of Australia* Inkata Press Melbourne

Willis J.H. (1963) *Victorian Toadstools and Mushrooms* 3rd ed Field Naturalist's Club of Victoria Melbourne

INDEX

GETTYSBURG COLLEGE

3326800 0381825 1

DATE DUE

Demco, Inc. 38-293